POVERTY AND THE STATE

POVERTY AND THE STATE

An Historical Sociology

TONY NOVAK

OPEN UNIVERSITY PRESS
MILTON KEYNES · PHILADELPHIA

Open University Press
Open University Educational Enterprises Limited
12 Cofferidge Close
Stony Stratford
Milton Keynes MK11 1BY, England

and

242 Cherry Street
Philadelphia, PA 19106, USA

First published 1988

British Library Cataloguing in Publication Data

Novak, Tony
  Poverty and the state : an historical sociology.
  1. Social security—Great Britain—History
  I. Title
  368.4′00941   HD7165

  ISBN 0-335-15545-6
  ISBN 0-335-15540-5 Pbk

Library of Congress Cataloging in Publication Data

Novak, Tony, 1950-
  Poverty and the state : an historical sociology/Tony Novak.
    p.   cm.
  Bibliography: p.
  Includes index.
  1. Social security—Great Britain—History.
  2. Public welfare—Great Britain—History.   I. Title
  HD7165.N682 1988
  361.6′50941—dc19   87-30161
                                                                CIP

  ISBN 0-335-15545-6   ISBN 0-335-15540-5 (pbk)

Typeset by Gilbert Composing Services
Printed in Great Britain by J.W. Arrowsmith Ltd., Bristol

CONTENTS

INTRODUCTION

It is over six hundred years since the state in Britain first intervened in the problem of poverty. Yet in all this time, and despite an immeasurably more wealthy society, poverty has not been eradicated. On the contrary, not only is poverty still with us, but in the last quarter of the twentieth century it is once again increasing.

The truth is that state intervention in the problem of poverty has never been intended to abolish poverty. It has rarely had the alleviation of poverty even as its primary aim. Rather, the system of social security has been developed to meet a set of economic and political objectives and constraints which set for it an entirely different agenda.

This book sets out, through both an historical and a contemporary analysis, to explore these constraints and objectives and their effects on the social security system as well as on the experience and extent of poverty. The need to understand what is going on at the moment is clear enough. One-third of the population of Britain lives in or on the margins of poverty, and one-quarter at or below the government's minimal level of Income Support. If nothing else, the misery that is inflicted by such poverty on millions of people demands attention. Yet not only is poverty increasing but the social security system is itself being refashioned in its wake to create a more rigid, more tightly controlled and meaner system of benefits.

The reasons for an historical approach are no less important. Society is not a static phenomenon; it is a constantly changing process of interaction, conflict and development. If we are to understand poverty, and in particular if we are to do something about it, we need to understand it within this process of change. We need to be aware of how and through what mechanisms change has taken place, what pitfalls have been faced in the past and what lessons are to be learned in overcoming them in the future.

The book begins with an analysis of the origins and nature of poverty. This is both a theoretical and an historical issue. Poverty is a product of capitalism. It both arose with the development of capitalism, and is continually created and recreated by it. The massive inequalities in income and wealth which capitalism creates are also inequalities on which it depends for its development and growth. One of the first lessons of history is that social structures and institutions are not immutable. Like the Roman Empire or the civilisation of the Aztecs, even capitalism had a beginning and will have an end. Another lesson is that many of the things we take for granted, or view as 'natural' or inevitable are themselves social products: the effects of generations if not centuries of getting used to a certain way of doing things. So it is with poverty. The poor have not always been with us; nor need they be in the future. The fact that they are still with us now requires us to understand the economic, social and political forces which maintain poverty in the midst of plenty.

The second chapter considers in more detail the principles by which the state has come to intervene in the problem of poverty. It does this through a specific examination of the 1834 Poor Law Amendment Act; perhaps the most significant piece of legislation in the history of the social security system. One of the lessons here is that seeing things such as poverty as 'inevitable' or natural did not come easily, but required – and continues to require – the active intervention of the state. The growth of capitalism itself depended in large part on the increasing power and regulation of the state in the creation of a labour market and in the reinforcement of the 'incentive to work'. The maintenance of poverty and inequality as the primary incentive to work has throughout history overshadowed all other considerations in the state's dealings with poverty. At the same time, state intervention has recognised that the maintenance of a grossly unequal society requires more than just the whip of poverty. It requires also the creation of a range of ideas and beliefs – about poverty, or wealth, or responsibility for unemployment, or the proper role of women – which legitimate and sanction the prevailing patterns of social inequality. It is in the creation of such ideologies that the social security system has played a central part.

The political balancing involved in the control and containment of poverty forms a major theme of the second part of the book, which focuses on the problem of unemployment and the development of social reform in the period immediately before the First World War. Unemployment today, and especially the growth of long-term unemployment, is a major cause of poverty. More than one in three of the unemployed have now been without work for over a year, yet of all claimants they remain on the lowest levels of benefit. At the same time, poverty is not confined to those excluded from the labour market; while unemployment has grown, so has the number of workers – a majority of them women – who earn their poverty. The growth in both forms of poverty are vitally connected; the threat of unemployment as a means of discipline and of wage restraint is something that has not disappeared with time.

Unemployment, however, while it serves important functions in a capitalist economy also presents a number of problems for capitalism. As William Beveridge once argued:

> the problem of unemployment lies, in a very special sense, at the root of most other social problems. Society is built upon labour; it lays upon its members responsibilities which in the vast majority of cases can only be met from the reward of labour.   (Beveridge 1909:1)

The third chapter examines the nature and causes of unemployment in late Victorian Britain, and the reasons why 'for the first time since the industrial revolution changed the very nature of industry, the problem of unemployment has become a political issue' (Jackson 1910:1).

The political challenge of unemployment, and of poverty, is what has determined the pace and development of social reform. As Chapter Four argues, the expansion of social security provision in the early part of this century was not inspired by humanitarian motives. Rather it was a response to, and sought to deal with, the threat of socialism and of a widespread working class hostility to a society and a state that was indifferent to the real welfare of working people. In attempting to meet this challenge, the state was to extend considerably its welfare activities. The main beneficiaries were not however the poorest, but that section of the working class – the organised male labour movement – which seemed to present the greatest threat.

The system of social security that was established before the First World War is one that in its fundamental structure remains to this day. The period since the end of the Second World War, however, has witnessed a continuing growth in its provision, as well as a massive expansion in other areas of state welfare activity. This post-war expansion of what became known as the welfare state, and the subsequent reaction by the new right against it, forms the focus of the remaining section of the book.

Chapter Five attempts to show that, while provision against poverty was to increase following the Second World War, the fundamental structures of inequality and poverty were to remain. Moreover, the particular social-democratic character of post-war governments until 1979 relied primarily upon the support of an electorate that was in work, increasingly better-off, overwhelmingly white and predominantly male. Women, black workers, the elderly, the unskilled and deskilled who formed the majority of the poor had to fight and struggle for their interests to be represented.

The impact of this struggle formed part of the crisis of capitalism that began to emerge in the 1970s. As the final chapter argues, this crisis has in part an economic dimension. The increasingly international nature of capitalism and changes in the structures of work and the labour market have been both a response to economic slump and have created new and growing dimensions of poverty. But the crisis of capitalism is also a political one, and the rise in the 1980s of right-wing governments in a number of western capitalist societies, including Britain, has witnessed an attempt to deal with this crisis; to break the power of organised labour and to reduce expectations of and demands on the state. The book thus finishes with an examination of poverty and social security under successive Conservative governments between 1979 and 1987.

Like most studies, this cannot claim to be an exhaustive or definitive account of poverty or of the state's response to it. Its central argument is that both the problem of poverty and the state's response to it are moulded by the requirements of a capitalist economy, and in particular by the need to maintain a wage labour market. It is this concern which dominates the social security system, even in its dealings with those who fall outside the labour market. Yet there are also other dynamics at work, which are not so readily identifiable as the simple product of a class society. Not least of these is the role of the social security system in maintaining a particular form of family structure in which the burden both of poverty and of caring for dependants falls most heavily on women. While this has increasingly been recognised, especially in accounts of poverty and social security in contemporary society, there is still considerable work to be done in discovering the historical roots and dynamics of a state provision which embodies a systematic gender bias.

Similarly there is a need to take further what could be called the geo-political dynamics of poverty. This book, for example, uses the term Britain, although strictly speaking it is more an account of poverty and the state in England. It does not, for example, address the special problems of poverty in Northern Ireland. With one-quarter of household income in Northern Ireland dependent upon social security benefits (compared with nine per cent in south east England), the dimensions of the Irish struggle take on a perspective which a fuller account of poverty and the British state would need to address. This is even more apparent when it is considered that Northern Ireland has for many years served as a testing ground for many of the policy initiatives of the British state, not only in methods of policing, but also in matters of social security (see Novak 1984:34). A similar argument can be made for Scotland, whose history and whose system and administration of social security benefits remains in certain important respects different from that of England.

Finally I would like to acknowledge the support, advice and encouragement given by Chris Jones in the completion of this book. If he has failed to influence this account to be sufficiently sensitive to the complexities and subtleties of poverty and political struggle, it will not be through want of trying.

part one

THE PROBLEM OF POVERTY

one

THE ORIGINS OF POVERTY

From feudalism to capitalism; the creation of wage labour; the growth of the state; 'reduced to mere hirelings'; poverty and wage labour; the wage system and poverty; poverty and the family wage; 'civilised' poverty.

Poverty as such begins with the tiller's freedom.
(Karl Marx *Grundrisse:* 735)

Despite the popular mythology, poverty has not always been with us. Throughout human history there has long been economic inequality, famine, shortage and distress. But poverty as we know it is a much more recent and historically specific phenomenon. It arises at a certain point in history, and is tied to a particular form of economic and social organisation. As the eighteenth-century historian Sir Frederick Eden argued in his book *The State of the Poor*:

> To the introduction of manufactures and the consequent emancipation of those who were dismissed by masters... I ascribe the introduction of a new class of men, henceforward described by the legislature under the denomination of *Poor*.
> (Eden 1796:57)

Poverty is not the same as inequality, although it is closely related to it. To be poor is not just to have less than others; it is also to be without the means of securing the necessary requirements of life. As Eden points out, poverty has its own specific historical origins, which in Britain first appeared in the thirteenth and fourteenth centuries with the decline of feudalism and the break-up of a system which, although unequal, offered everyone the opportunity to secure their own subsistence. In short, the origins of poverty lie in the origins of capitalism, and if we are fully to understand poverty we have first to understand the dynamics of capitalism.

From feudalism to capitalism

All societies, as forms of human social organisation, depend upon human labour for survival: on labour to produce those goods such as food, clothing and shelter which maintain human existence, as well as on the labour, the nurturing and care, that reproduces future generations.

In the most primitive societies, the labour involved in production was direct; requiring simply the daily gathering of food provided by nature. But as human society evolved, so a part of this daily labour was used, not for immediate consumption, but for the production of tools. With such 'means of production' a given amount of labour could produce a great deal more. More land, to take a simple example, could be dug with a spade than with bare hands or with a stick, and so the productivity of labour correspondingly increased.

It is this growth in the means of production that holds the key to economic growth and expansion. The greater the means of production, whether in the form of simple tools, more sophisticated machinery, factories or industrial complexes, the greater the productivity of labour, and the greater the wealth that any society can produce. What distinguishes one type of society from another – slavery from feudalism, or feudalism from capitalism – are the conditions under which this production is carried out. For in all but the most primitive societies, the social organisation of production has been characterised by a division between a minority who own and a majority who do not own the means of producing wealth: between slave-owner and slave, lord and peasant, employer and worker.

While it is this fundamental division of society into social classes according to their relationship to the means of production that is the basis for Marx's observation that 'the history of all hitherto existing society is the history of class struggle', the mechanism of its operation has differed from one type of society to another. Slaves, for example, do not own land, but neither do they own even their own bodies, for both are the property of the slave-owner. Under feudalism, on the other hand, the peasantry had direct access to and control over the means of production – principally the land – and were able to produce for themselves.

It was this arrangement that enabled the feudal ruling class to take the surplus of peasant production. Through the use of force and the sanction of custom, religious belief and superstition they demanded tithes, dues and services, payable in kind or in compulsory labour, and later in the form of taxes and rents paid in money. But their ability to do so depended first and foremost on the ability of the peasantry to maintain and produce for itself. The wealth of the feudal ruling class was obtained not so much by the direct economic exploitation of the peasantry, but by its political exploitation; the seizure of the surplus produced by the peasantry over and above their immediate needs.

The development of capitalism from within the structure of feudal society was to challenge and ultimately overthrow this relationship. For whereas feudalism depended upon the direct access to and control over the means of production by those who produced its wealth – the peasantry to the land, or artisans over their tools and equipment – capitalism depends upon their separation. Within a capitalist economy, workers do not own or control the means of production – the factories or offices they work in, or the tools and machines they work with – instead they sell their labour-power to those who do own the means of production in return for a wage.

The accumulation of wealth under capitalism is, unlike feudalism, a direct result of this economic relationship. For in buying labour-power the capitalist buys a very special commodity. Unlike the other commodities – the raw materials, machines or factories – needed for production, labour alone is capable of increasing wealth; of turning raw materials like wood or iron ore into something useful like a chair or a plane. In buying this unique commodity of labour-power, employers buy the ability of labour to produce more than it consumes. As we have seen, the greater the means of production – the tools and machines created by past labour – with which current labour works, the more that it can produce, and the greater the surplus created over and above its own immediate needs. Since however under capitalism what is produced by labour does not belong to those who produce it, but to those who employ them, this surplus is taken by the owners of the means of production as their own private property, and is then used both to buy further labour-power and to increase the means of production for the future. As Eden recognised:

> It is not the possession of land, or of money, but the command of labour, which the various circumstances of society places more or less within their disposal, that distinguishes the opulent from the labouring part of the community.
>
> (Eden 1796:2)

The creation of wage labour

The 'various circumstances' which placed the labour-power of the majority of the population within the disposal of a minority did not appear miraculously or spontaneously, but were the product of a long and hard-fought development. The creation of a market in human labour required above all else the creation of a class of people – a working class – who had no means of survival other than selling their labour, and no alternative other than to do so.

It was to take many hundreds of years for this transformation to be effected, for the peasantry to be uprooted from the soil and made to be dependent upon waged labour for survival. The extinction of feudalism in Britain and its replacement by a system of capitalist production and wage labour was a long process full of conflict. The two systems were antagonistic, and the conditions for the growth of one – the creation of a free labour market, the institution of private ownership of property, and the economic and social ideologies that accompanied it – were the negation of the conditions for the existence of the other. Although capitalism was to achieve its full status with the industrial revolution in Britain, the foundations for it had already been well laid beforehand in the transformation brought about by the development of capitalist production in agriculture.

From the twelfth century onwards money, rather than barter, as a means of exchange began to infiltrate feudal Britain, as too did production for a market rather than just for subsistence. Neither money nor production for a market were in themselves defining characteristics of capitalism, but they provided the incentive to a number of the feudal lords to transform the nature of feudal production; to fence off and enclose the land as their own private property, and to evict the smaller peasants and tenants from their holdings.

It was this growing separation of a serf and peasant population from the means of production, and the introduction of a system of wage labour, that marks the beginnings of capitalism and the origins of poverty. As Marx argued, poverty began with the tiller's 'freedom':

> When... the great English landowners dismissed their re-tainers who had, with them, consumed the surplus product of the land; when further their tenants chased off the smaller cottagers, etc., then... a mass of living labour power was thrown onto the labour market, a mass which was free in a double sense, free from the old relations of clientship, bondage and servitude, and secondly free of all belongings and possessions, and of every objective, material form of being, free of all property; dependent on the sale of its labour capacity or on begging, vagabondage and robbery as its only source of income.
>
> (Marx 1974: 507)

The 'emancipation' of feudal society was double-edged: it meant freedom from feudal servitude and oppression – and this was to be the rallying-point for the great series of peasant revolts during the fifteenth and sixteenth centuries – but for many 'freedom' also meant to be cut adrift from the land, from the principal means of production; it meant to be left suspended over a bottomless chasm of destitution; in short, it meant poverty.

Over the course of some three hundred years this steadily growing pool of 'free' labour created by the break-up of feudalism was to provide an indispensable condition for the development and growth of capitalism. The eviction of the peasantry and the dismissal of the great retinues of feudal serfs and retainers did not, however, mean that those who were dispossessed could necessarily find employment for their labour. Still less did it mean that they would choose to do so: that having escaped the slavery of feudalism, they would exchange it for the life of a wage-slave. On the one hand, the development of capitalism was a very uneven process; its demand for labour fluctuated greatly, and did not necessarily correspond to the numbers of those thrown onto the labour market. On the other, the alternative between wage labour and starvation was not always so starkly posed; there was still then, and until the enclosure movement reached its height during the eighteenth century, free and common land to settle on, until the introduction of the Game Laws (which by the eighteenth century accounted for one in seven of all criminal prosecutions) there was still wild game to be caught, and, until the Reformation, the charity of the monasteries to help provide a subsistence.

The failure of the new class of dispossessed poor to provide a willing supply of labour, and their preference to search out a living in other ways, was to evoke an increasingly hostile reaction from the feudal state. It was in many respects in its attempts to deal with the problem of poverty and to create a machinery for doing so that the machinery of the state was formed. In 1349 the Statute of Labourers – the first of the English Poor Laws – was passed. Coming in the wake of the Black Death, a bubonic plague that had swept Europe and is estimated to have killed nearly half the population, the statute, noting the 'great scarcity of servants', and in particular the fact that 'some will not serve unless they may receive excessive wages, and some rather willing to be in idleness than by labour to get their living', ordered that:

> every man and woman of our realm of England . . . not living in merchandise, nor exercising any craft, nor having of his own whereof he may live, nor proper land . . . and not serving any other . . . shall be bounden to serve him which so shall him require.
>
> (23 Edward III. Cited de Schweinitz 1947:28)

For feudal governments, the emergence of poverty was a threat: a threat in that 'free' labour undermined the existing structures of feudalism and added fuel to the discontent of the peasantry, and a threat in that the poor and dispossessed themselves, especially with the disbanding of the private armies of the nobility that came with the increasing power of the monarchy, represented a serious and growing problem of social and political disorder:

The action of the central government was dictated by fear.

Every Tudor monarch had to contend with at least one serious rising, and, not insignificantly, every decade from the 1530s onwards saw at least one Act directed towards the relief of the poor and the suppression of vagrancy.

(Pound 1973:82)

Up until the mid-seventeenth century, when feudalism (in England if not in Britain as a whole) was finally to be overthrown, attempts were made to slow the development of capitalism, to limit the creation of poverty and to contain the problem of the poor. Legislation sought to restrict the enclosure of land, to limit the amount of wages that could be paid, to forbid the daily hiring of labour, to fix minimum yearly periods of hire, and to restrict the movement of labourers so as to prevent them moving about the country. In 1589, for example, it was forbidden to build any house unless it had four acres of land attached, to build a house within three miles of London except for those with over £5 in goods or £3 in land, to take in lodgers, or to subdivide houses into tenements; 'evidently', writes Hasbach, 'to guard against the development of a proletarian class of day-labourers' (Hasbach 1908:41).

Such attempts were, however, to prove futile. So too ultimately did the increasingly violent attempts by successive governments to prevent the growth of the poor by re-imposing servitude on those who had escaped the social relations of feudalism. During the reign of Henry VII, for example, it was enacted that the punishment for 'loitering, wandering and idleness' was 'to be tied to the end of a cart naked and be beaten with whips till his body be bloody ... and to return to the place where he was born ... and there put himself to labour like a true man oweth to do'. In 1536 legislation decreed that a second offence meant that the offender should be 'not only whipped again ... but also shall have the upper part of the gristle of his right ear clean cut off'. By 1547 it was ordered that:

If any man or woman, able to work, should refuse to labour, and live idly for three days, that he or she should be branded with a red-hot iron on the breast with the letter V, and should be adjudged the slave, for two years, of any person who should inform against such idler.

Any attempt to escape from slavery during this period would lead to that person being made a slave for life, whilst anyone guilty of a second attempt to escape, 'shall have judgement to suffer pains and execution of death as a felon and as enemies of the Commonwealth'. It was through such means that Britain's supposedly 'free' labour force was created, and on such foundations that capitalism was built. Such measures also form the historical basis for Britain's system of social security provision, and its continuing obsession with the maintenance of the labour market.

The growth of the state

The attempts by the feudal monarchy to deal with the problem of the poor played an important part in the growing centralisation of political authority and in the emergence of what we now know as the state. In a literal sense, the state grew out of the household of the feudal monarchy, which in its attempts to exercise power over a feuding nobility gradually extended its apparatus of national political control. In a more fundamental sense, however, the state represents a particular set of social relations: an attempt to maintain a particular economic and social formation. In this respect, the state reflects the interests of the dominant class in society: the maintenance of the existing order becomes the maintenance of those relationships and ideologies which are conducive to the interests of that class. The emergence of the problem of poverty, and the subsequent attempts by the feudal ruling class to control and contain it, marked the beginning of state 'social policy': of the state's active regulation of social life. No longer concerned only with military affairs, with the appointment of Justices of the Peace as its local administrative agents, 'national regulation and control of labour became one of the more important of the new functions of government' (Hill 1952: 37).

Ironically, such attempts by successive feudal monarchs and their allies to restrain the growth of capitalism and limit its destabilising effects had in almost every respect the opposite effect. To the extent that the Poor Laws, in their attempts to suppress the growth of the poor, succeeded in driving the propertyless onto the labour market, they added to the growing strength of capitalism. To the extent that the feudal monarchy was successful in limiting the spread of capitalism or placing restrictions on its growth, it further antagonised that section of the ruling class that had forsaken its feudal responsibilities in favour of a commercial future. Indeed the ruling class was itself becoming increasingly differentiated. Out of its midst had grown an increasingly powerful class of merchants, landlords, farmers and manufacturers, whose wealth depended on their ability (or the ability of their tenants or suppliers) to secure a plentiful supply of cheap labour. To them, restrictions on the growth of the labour market were increasingly unacceptable.

By the reign of Elizabeth I the rearguard action of the feudal state against the rising forces of capital was to reach its height. By then the scale of the problem – the growing number of dispossessed, the uncertainties and fluctuations of capitalist employment, and increasing economic and political instability – had reached such proportions that the outright repression of the poor was no longer tenable. In 1572 a compulsory 'poor rate' was levied on all owners of property, to provide relief for those who could not work. Subsequently the Justices of the Peace were ordered also to purchase materials from the poor rates and to provide work for the able-bodied unemployed.

In 1601 the Elizabethan statutes were re-codified under what was to become known as the Elizabethan Poor Law – the '43rd of Elizabeth' which was thereafter to become a rallying-point for working class demands for the right to relief and the 'right to work' – establishing a system of relief and of parish employment for those unable to obtain their own subsistence. Although not formally repealed until 1948, its practical history was, however, short-lived.

Developed in the attempt to deal with the new problem of poverty, the Poor Law had, by the beginning of the seventeenth century, come to reflect the interests and concerns of those who controlled the apparatus of state. To them, poverty was a threat: the product of an economic system that had grown up within feudalism, and which now threatened to destroy the social fabric. In the attempt to meet this problem the feudal state under the rule of an absolute monarchy had developed a variety of measures and means of control to halt the spread of poverty and vagrancy, to suppress the growth of a 'free' population, and increasingly, through controls on prices and production, to restrict and restrain the development of capitalism.

Such attempts were to prove futile. The coercion and control of 'free' labour had itself contributed to the establishment of a market in labour-power on which the growth of capitalism depended. By the time that the Elizabethan state began to get to grips with the problem through the provision of public, rather than private, employment of the poor, and the regulation and control of prices and markets, it was already too late. The feudal state ruled over a society which was essentially no longer feudal but increasingly capitalist, and in which the representatives of the new forces of capital had already achieved economic and considerable political power. So long as state policy had coincided with their interests, the owners of capital had been content to endure an alliance with their feudal host. But as this policy began to come into conflict with their interests, so the state came to be seen as an obstacle to their development. 'The chief consequence of the crown's policy', argues Barrington Moore, 'was to an-tagonise those who upheld the right to do what one liked ... with one's own property' (Moore 1969:14).

By the seventeenth century the real relations of property in Britain had been transformed, and the developing forces of capital brought into conflict with the surviving social relations of feudal production as embodied in the state. The contradictions inherent within the co-existence of two opposing forms of economic and social organisation could no longer be contained, and in the mid-seventeenth century broke out in the form of Civil War. The overthrow of the monarchy, although later reinstated, marked more than just an internal conflict within the ruling class, for it signified the demise of feudalism in Britain and the ascendancy of capitalism as the dominant mode of production. As Marx and Engels were later to argue:

> The means of production and exchange, on whose foundation the bourgeoisie built itself up, were generated in feudal society. At a certain stage in the development of these means of production and exchange, the conditions under which feudal society produced and exchanged, the feudal organisation of agriculture and manufacturing industry, in one word, the feudal relations of property became no longer compatible with

the already developed productive forces; they became so many fetters. They had to be burst asunder; they were burst asunder.

(Marx and Engels 1968:40)

'Reduced to mere hirelings'

The period from the Civil War to the advent of the industrial revolution was to be the 'golden age' of capitalist agriculture in Britain, and through this was to lay the foundations for the emergence in Britain of industrial capitalism. In breaking the power of the monarchy and replacing it by the power of an essentially capitalist landowning aristocracy in Parliament, the Civil War had swept away the barriers to the enclosure movement and the 'modernisation' of agriculture. Similarly many of the other restrictions that the feudal state had placed in the way of capitalist development fell into disuse. In the matter of poor relief the initiative fell away from central government to the 15,000 separate parishes which divided the country, and each was more or less left to determine its own policy in accordance with its local labour needs and political complexion.

While the Civil War broke the power of the feudal aristocracy, it did not, as in the case of the French revolution of 1789, break the aristocracy as a class. In many respects there was no need to do so, since many of them had already allied themselves with the new forces of capital, and have (unlike many other capitalist countries) ever since retained a position of power and influence within the British ruling class. Still less did the Civil War break decisively the established ideologies of feudalism. Puritanism and the Protestant ethic were to be the cutting-edge of capitalist ideology – with their emphasis on hard work, abstinence and the view that individuals alone were responsible for their own destinies. But in this the new ideology had to take battle with established religion and morality, and its views of a static society in which people's position in the social structure was fixed by divine order, and in which property had obligations towards the poor.

By the end of the seventeenth century, however, a chorus of voices was to be raised against the view that poverty was the result of economic circumstance, and that the poor had a right to expect relief from the rich. According to John Locke:

> If the cause of the evil be looked into, we humbly conceive it will be found to have proceeded neither from a scarcity of provision, nor from a want of employment for the poor, since the goodness of God has blessed these times with plenty... The growth of the poor must have some other cause, and it can be nothing else but a relaxation of discipline and a corruption of manners.
>
> (Cited Marshall 1926:31)

Or as Daniel Defoe argued in 1704:

> 'Tis the men that won't work, not the men that can get no work, which makes the number of our poor ... What is needed is a regulation of the poor in England, not a setting them to work.
>
> (Cited de Schweinitz 1947:59)

At one level, the employers of labour found the practice of parish employment of the poor to be in competition with their own requirements for labour. But perhaps even more fundamentally, the relief of poverty itself was seen as weakening the incentive to work. During the build-up to the industrial revolution, the problem of labour discipline was to be posed, and confronted, in an increasingly open form. The success of capitalism depended not merely on the physical creation of a working class, but on instilling the necessary discipline and commitment to wage labour. In this, and from an early stage, employers faced the problem that money as an incentive to work was often insufficient. As one observer noted:

> It has been remarked by our clothiers and manufacturers that when corn has been cheap they have had great difficulty to get their spinning and other work done. For the poor could buy provisions enough with two or three days wages to serve them a week, and would spend the rest in idleness, drinking etc. But when corn has been dear, they have been forced to stick all the week at it.
>
> (Cited Marshall 1926:32)

Similar complaints were and have continued to be made about the lack of motivation and discipline – the seemingly inexplicable failure to respond to the lure of consumerism and market forces – amongst the young, amongst black workers and others (see, for example, Davies 1986; Gilroy 1987). In pre-industrial England, as E.P. Thompson and others have demonstrated, for a population accustomed to work that varied with the weather and the seasons, that involved some degree of control over how and what was produced, factory life dictated by the pace of the machine and the clock was anathema. Moreover, without the stimulus of advertising and consumerism, the chains of hire purchase and debt, fluctuations in the cost of subsistence were readily reflected in a refusal on the part of workers to sell their labour. As another writer remarked:

> Our populace have adopted a notion that, as Englishmen, they enjoy a birthright privilege of being more free and independent than in any country in Europe. Now this idea, as far as it affects the bravery of our troops, may be of some use; but the less the manufacturing poor have of it, certainly the better for themselves and the state ... It is extremely dangerous to encourage mobs in a commercial state like ours, where, perhaps, seven parts out of eight of the whole, are people with little or no property. The cure will not be perfect till our manufacturing poor are contented to labour six days for the same sum which they now earn in four.
>
> (Cited Marx 1974: 262)

In the absence of such a 'cure', many of the early factories — including that of the supposed philanthropist Robert Owen — were to rely upon the indentured labour of adult paupers and children (Redford 1926:26). Within the factories themselves, new systems of timekeeping and of fines for lateness or absenteeism were introduced (cf Pollard 1963; Thompson 1967; Hobsbawm 1967). But perhaps the most potent 'cure' was the combination of a growing population, the continuing 'modernisation' of agriculture, with its enclosure of land and the application of machinery, and a rising level of inflation. By the end of the eighteenth century, the creation of a propertyless proletariat (although one that was still predominantly rural rather than urban) was practically complete. As Arthur Young then observed:

> Formerly many of the lower sort of people occupied tenements of their own, with parcels of land about them. On these they

raised a considerable part of their subsistence, without being obliged, as now, to buy all they want at shops. But since these small parcels of ground have been swallowed up in the contiguous farms and enclosures, and as cottages themselves have been pulled down, and the families which used to occupy them are crowded together in decayed farmhouses with hardly enough ground about them for a cabbage garden, and being thus reduced to mere hirelings, they are very liable to come to want.

(Cited Hasbach 1908:129)

To be thus 'reduced to mere hirelings' was the essence of agricultural 'improvement'. The development of capitalism in agriculture created a working class, on a scale unparalleled in the rest of the world, that was to provide the labour-power for the growth of industrial capitalism in Britain. As John Saville has argued:

Nowhere save in Britain was the peasantry virtually eliminated before the acceleration of economic growth that is associated with the development of industrial capitalism, and of the many special features of early industrialisation in Britain, none is more striking than the presence of a rapidly growing proletariat in the countryside.

(Saville 1969:250)

The formation of a working class was an achievement that had been created through much hardship and suffering; that had involved the use of force in a variety of guises, whether in the form of open coercion, the use of the power of the state, or the economic weapon of hunger. It was, however, a process that had not been achieved easily. In particular, it had met with fierce and sustained opposition from the poor themselves who had fought against the process of proletarianisation, had resisted being turned into mere commodities, and engaged in widespread and popular struggles against the encroachments of capitalism and the market system (see, eg, Thompson 1974). To create a working class in a physical sense – to uproot the peasantry and make them dependent upon wage labour – was only part of the requirements of the development of capitalism. To secure their attachment to wage labour, to present this system as natural or at least inevitable, and to deal with the consequences of poverty, was, and remains, an equally difficult task.

Poverty and wage labour

The association of poverty with wage labour is more than just a matter of historical curiosity. During the course of the twentieth century the advanced capitalist nations have increased their wealth and productive power to an unprecedented degree. Living standards have similarly risen to offer all the inhabitants of these countries a range of goods and services that would have been unthinkable a hundred or even fifty years earlier. The engine of capitalist growth and accumulation has since the industrial revolution achieved stunning success. Yet within this remarkable achievement, poverty has not disappeared; nor is its persistence marginal or temporary. Today in Britain it is estimated that one-third of the population live in or on the margins of poverty, facing a dull and unremitting struggle to maintain a minimum level of subsistence. Inequalities in both income and wealth remain as entrenched as ever, and having narrowed slightly in the two or three decades after the Second World War have in the 1980s begun once again to widen. The costs in terms of human suffering are only barely reflected in the growing statistics of premature death, suicide and chronic ill-health (see, eg, Townsend and Davidson 1982).

At the same time the latter half of the twentieth century has seen the spectre of famine, mass starvation and malnutrition increasing within countries of the so-called Third World. The tragedies of Ethiopia or the Sudan have within the west become only the visible tip of an iceberg of chronic poverty and destitution throughout Africa, south and central America and Asia. There, crowded into sprawling shanty towns that encircle many of the great cosmopolitan cities, the new poor of the Third World, uprooted from the land on which they previously gained their subsistence, flock in search of employment, mirroring in a single generation the experience of the creation of a working class in Britain over centuries.

The contrast between poverty in the Third World and poverty in a country like Britain has led many people to believe and to argue that the two cannot be compared: that they are different not merely in matters of degree, but that they are qualitatively different things. It has further led some to argue that there is no longer any 'real' poverty in Britain, that, in the words of Patrick Jenkin, Secretary of State for Social Services under the Conservative government in 1980, 'the harsh, grinding poverty that disfigured the 1920s and 1930s has gone' and that to talk of continuing and relative poverty in an affluent society like Britain's is not only mistaken but 'absurd' (*Hansard* 15th April 1980).

It is of course undeniable that the standard of living of the least well-off in Britain far exceeds that of their Third World counterparts, just as it is equally true that many Third World countries contain a ruling class whose wealth is spectacular even by western standards. It is also the case, as Lenin argued, that the higher standard of living, even of the poor, in the west is in part achieved at the expense of Third World hunger. Yet poverty in the advanced capitalist nations and poverty in the Third World are not fundamentally different things, for underlying both is the structure of inequality, of the private ownership of wealth and the system of wage labour, that is the inescapable feature of capitalism. By way of illustration, we have only to remove the social security system in Britain, to take away the effects of state intervention and consider solely what the market economy provides, to discover that the poorest twenty per cent of the British population would in 1982 have had an average income of less than 50p a week. When viewed in these terms, the poverty of the Third World is not so very far away.

Behind this chasm of potential destitution and starvation, relieved only by the transfer of income to the very poorest by the state, lies the inherent inequalities of capitalism. In Britain, as in all capitalist societies, the ownership of property is highly concentrated. Five per cent of the population own 41 per cent of all marketable wealth, and one quarter of the population owns over 80 per cent. Moreover, such statistics include all property, such as consumer durables and housing. When the distribution of wealth is looked at in the form of 'productive' wealth – wealth in the form of capital and means of production such as factories or offices – we find that a tiny 3½ per cent of the population owns 90 per cent of all private company stocks and shares, and 96 per cent of privately-owned land. For such people, work is not an economic necessity. Their very ownership of wealth provides them with a source of income.

Those without wealth, however, must seek an income through wage labour. If they fail to do so they face the prospect of destitution. It is this fundamental lack of economic security that defines poverty, and which remains the ultimate incentive to work. It is, in the final analysis, the threat which keeps people at the machine or in the office. It is in the attempt to escape it that people seek work, but it is a threat from which most people can never fully escape. The reality of poverty is that each week workers have again to sell their labour in order to get the means to live. As the nineteenth-century political economist Patrick Colquhoun argued:

> Poverty is that state and condition in society where the individual has no surplus labour in store, and, consequently, no property but what is derived from the constant exercise of industry in the various occupations of life; or in other words, it is the state of every one who must labour for subsistence.
>
> (Cited Rose 1971:47)

Poverty, thus defined, is not simply the consequence of capitalist production (a mal-distribution of resources that can be corrected given sufficient will), but is an essential precondition for the existence of capitalism. As Colquhoun went on to argue:

> Poverty is therefore a most necessary and indispensable ingredient in society, without which nations and communities could not exist in a state of civilisation. It is the lot of man, it is the source of wealth, since without poverty there would be no labour, and without labour there could be no riches, no refinement, no comfort, and no benefit to those who may be possessed of wealth.
>
> (ibid)

It is the fundamental economic insecurity of wage labour that lies behind and alone can explain modern poverty. When social scientists talk of old age, sickness, unemployment and even large families as 'causes' of poverty, they mystify this underlying relationship. Such factors do not in themselves 'cause' poverty. It is quite possible to be old, sick, without paid employment and to be extremely rich. To be too old or sick or unable to find work results in poverty only for those for whom work is an economic necessity. Poverty is thus first and foremost a function of class. It is the product of an economic system which is based not simply on inequality but on a fundamental division between the owners and producers of social wealth, and which requires the maintenance of poverty as a spur to its system of wage labour.

The wage system and poverty

The wage system and poverty are inextricably related. The relationship between wages and poverty is not however exhausted by the recognition that those who fail to earn a wage face destitution and deprivation; nor is it sufficient additionally to take account of the fact that for many workers – currently one-third of the adult workforce – the wages received are insufficient to maintain an adequate standard of living: a feature of poverty which often is neglected. Rather, an understanding of the wage system is crucial for an understanding of the way in which we have come to define and measure poverty.

It is only over the course of the past hundred years, and more for political than scientific reasons, that social scientists have attempted to define poverty as a certain level of income: a 'line' below which people are poor, and above which they are not. Before then, as the nineteenth-century political economist and reformer Nassau Senior noted, there was an 'unfortunate double meaning of the word *poor*...'

> In one sense of the word it means merely the aggregate of the individuals who... are really unable to earn their own subsistence... In its widest [sic] acceptation it is opposed to the word *rich*; and in its most common use it includes all except the higher and middle classes.
>
> (Senior 1865:67)

The shift from seeing poverty as the condition of existence of a class, which took place at the end of the nineteenth century, to a definition of poverty as a certain level of income has played a major part in the de-politicisation of poverty. It has also led to debate about the measurement and extent of poverty: about whether poverty is an absolute or relative phenomenon, and about the number of people that are to be considered as

The notion that poverty is absolute, that there is a universal minimum level of subsistence that is required for human survival, is one that would find few strict adherents. There are, of course, many who would argue that there is an 'absolute' level of subsistence necessary for survival in a country like Britain, but such a claim already reveals the relative nature of poverty: that what is necessary for human beings to live will vary from one society to another, just as it varies within any one society over time. Even attempts to fix an 'absolute' level of poverty by reference solely to the nutritional requirements for physiological survival fall against the fact that what is necessary simply to survive in Britain in the 1980s where the average life expectancy is over 70 is greater than what it was a hundred years ago when life expectancy was much lower.

Measured poverty must always be relative, since what it is measuring is a social product which changes both over time and from one society to another. The point at issue simply becomes what it is relative to. In Britain, it is conventional to take the level of Income Support, previously known as Supplementary Benefit, as the measurement of poverty. One of the problems of this is that it is open to any government to reduce the level of benefit, and thereby to reduce the number of people defined as being in poverty, without any change at all in material circumstances. It is thus a largely arbitrary level, set more often than not by what governments feel they can get away with in the form of minimum levels of benefit to the poor.

The minimum standard of living for its citizens that any government can get away with may indeed be one definition of poverty, and certainly more useful than some. It at least points to the fact that conceptions of poverty are socially created, rather than measured by some external yardstick. If we are to arrive at a better conception of what constitutes and creates a minimum acceptable standard of living however we need to do so with reference to the way in which living standards are created and defined. In other words, we need to do so with reference to wages.

The payment that is made for the purchase of labour-power, like other commodities, reflects what it costs to produce: what it costs for workers to maintain themselves and their future generations. Taken as a whole, wages represent the cost of subsistence of the working class. But labour is a human commodity: what it costs to produce varies from country to country, and from one period to another. Living standards are not fixed, but rise with a rise in productive power. With this rises also what counts as a minimum standard of living. As even the eighteenth-century writer Arthur Young recognised:

> Everyone but an idiot knows that the lower classes must be kept poor or they will never be industrious; I do not mean that the poor of England are to be kept like the poor of France, but, the state of the country considered, they must (like all mankind) be in poverty or they will not work.
>
> (Cited Furniss 1965:118)

The level of subsistence – the level at which earlier economists defined the poverty of the working class – is a fluctuating and relative level. As Marx argued:

> His means of subsistence must...be sufficient to maintain him in his normal state as a labouring individual. His natural wants, such as food, clothing, fuel and housing, vary according to the climatic and other physical conditions of the country. On the other hand, the number and extent of his so-called necessary wants, as also the modes of satisfying them, are themselves the product of historical development, and depend therefore to a great extent on the degree of civilisation of a country, more particularly on the habits and degree of comfort in which the class of free labourers has been formed.
>
> (Marx 1974:168)

Needs are socially defined, and what is considered necessary for subsistence will vary from time to time and from one society to another. This is not an arbitrary development. Within capitalism, the standard of living of workers is determined by their wages, and wages in turn represent the cost of labour, or rather the cost of the maintenance and reproduction of labour: of what is necessary to maintain the workforce and its future generation. Unlike other commodities, however, the cost of human labour is a reflection not only of economic but also of social and political forces. The increasing wealth of society introduces new needs, which in turn raise the requirements of life:

Capital can only increase by exchanging itself for labour-power, by calling wage-labour to life. The labour-power of the wage worker can only be exchanged for capital by increasing capital ... The faster capital intended for production, productive capital, increases, the more, therefore, industry prospers, the more the bourgeoisie enriches itself and the better business is, the more workers does the capitalist need, and the more dearly does the worker sell himself. The indispensable condition for a tolerable condition for the worker is, therefore, the fastest possible growth of productive capital ... When productive capital grows, the demand for labour grows; consequently, the price of labour, wages, goes up.

(Marx 1968:83)

It is this growth in capital, in the productive power and wealth of society, that raises the relative level of subsistence. In doing so it sets new levels of what constitutes a minimum acceptable standard of life. The average wage represents this level of subsistence. Of course, many workers are paid below the average, some receive no wages at all, whilst others are paid above the average. But, as a whole, the greater the productivity of labour, the greater the accumulation of capital, and the greater the level of subsistence.

Even so, while wages (and thus living standards) have increased through past centuries, it is a remarkable feature of capitalism that throughout this time the share of wages in the gross national product has remained virtually constant. Thus while real wages have increased, relative wages – relative to the amount of wealth produced – have remained more or less the same. In 1860, wages represented 38.7 per cent of GNP; in 1960 37.8 per cent (Feinstein 1968). The truth is of course that wages do not rise spontaneously: a rise in wages has always to be struggled and fought for as wealth increases, just as employers seek to keep wages down so as to increase the size of the surplus value that labour creates. Nevertheless, one thing which is clear is that the level at which subsistence is defined rises with a rise in wages. It is not, as is often argued, that gains made by those in work are made at the expense of the poor; on the contrary, all the evidence of history points to the material gains of the working class as the only guarantee of a rising standard of living for all.

Any attempt to 'measure' poverty must be seen in this context;

just as any attempt to define it must recognise that poverty, like wealth, is relative and is a social creation. It is certainly useful, and politically very important to have a measure of the degree and extent of poverty in any society, but the decision as to where this measure is to be taken can only be made with respect to wages, and thus to living standards and the development of wealth. The decision in Britain in 1980 only to increase benefits in line with prices, and not wages, thus constituted a major setback for the poor.

Yet the elaboration of a 'poverty line', while useful in estimating the number of people living below that level, is itself fraught with difficulty and hides as much as it reveals. Poverty is much more than just a level of income; it also involves questions of power and lack of choice. To see poverty simply as a standard of living – even assuming there is agreement about where that line is to be drawn – fails to recognise that poverty is a continuum stretching throughout the working class. This continuum is not only one that means that it becomes impossible to draw a line, below which people are poor, and slightly above which they suddenly are not; nor is it simply a case of recognising that most working people, at some time in their lives, will fall below the sociological measurement of poverty. It is a continuum that is set by the common and ever-present threat of poverty: an experience that is in part defined by living standards, but that much more fundamentally is set by the insecurity of dependence on wage labour. Poverty has thus to be seen in the context of class: in the context of a society divided between those who own nothing but their labour-power and those who own the means of producing wealth, and who thus command the livelihood of the majority.

Poverty and the family wage

Before we leave the examination of wages, there is one further point to be considered. In principle, capitalism depends upon 'free' labour: workers that are unencumbered by property, and who have constantly to sell their labour-power to survive. In practice, however, whilst capitalism is the dominant mode of production in the world, it is not the only mode of production. Indeed, throughout its development it has incorporated other modes of production and various forms of 'unfree' labour within itself and used them to its advantage. Such is evident, for example, in the ways that peasant and subsistence production within the Third World has become tied into an international capitalist economy, as also in the use of migrant labour employed in the capitalist economies, but whose costs of maintenance and reproduction are borne by the subsistence economies in the countries from which they came and to which they are subsequently returned.

A similar process is also evident in the manner in which the growth of capitalism has incorporated what may be called the 'domestic economy' and the unpaid and unfree labour of women. Before the advent of capitalism, all production took place within the household, where the making of goods such as clothes or furniture or the growing and preparation of food all counted towards survival. With the advent of wage labour, and especially the introduction of factories, however, part of this work was moved outside of the domestic economy and into the market economy. Waged work became 'real' work; the work that remained within the domestic economy, by implication, was not. Yet it was, and remains, necessary work: the labour involved in bringing up children, in caring for the sick or in the multitude of tasks that make up housework is as necessary for human survival and comfort as the labour involved in producing cars or aeroplanes. Moreover, to the extent that this domestic labour remained outside the market economy, and thus unpaid, it has enabled capital to reduce the cost of subsistence of its paid workforce. Workers, after all, cannot eat a wage packet: the unpaid domestic labour, provided mostly by women, that goes into turning a wage into the means of subsistence is thus turned indirectly to the benefit of capital, whose wage costs are correspondingly reduced. From the point of view of capital, the perpetuation of this domestic economy, and of women's place within it, remains as we shall see a central priority.

It is from this inter-relationship between the wage system and domestic life that many people have argued for recognition of a 'family wage', and see in it a solution to the problem of poverty amongst dependent women and children. In one sense, of course, the wages that capital pays out already do represent a sort of family wage: for it is on the total sum of the wages paid out that both workers and their dependants have to survive. This is not of course to say that such wages are sufficient, even in general, to maintain working class living standards, and the attempt to do so has been one factor in the growing number of previously dependent and married women seeking paid employment. Increasingly over the past thirty years or so it has taken two wage earners within a household to maintain a rising standard of living.

Still less is it true that any particular wage is adequate for any particular family. The wage system takes no account of an individual worker's responsibilities and commitments: within any one branch of employment the same wage is paid to a single person as is paid to one with dependants to support, and any further readjustment is left to the state through its systems of taxation and benefits. Here, the state's concern both not to undermine work incentives and not to weaken what it has regarded as the responsibilities of women and the family have greatly circumscribed and limited its role. The reality of family poverty – that in the late 1980s one-third of all children grow up in conditions of severe deprivation – is one that only a fundamental challenge to the wage system can relieve.

'Civilised' poverty

The threat of poverty is a threat that hangs over the heads of all those who have to sell their labour to survive. This ultimately is true even of the more prosperous and salaried 'middle class' which has grown to considerable proportions, especially during the present century. Although often enjoying a higher standard of living, with easier conditions of work and greater security of employment, together with the protection of private pension schemes to see them through old age, they too are no more than a few weeks removed from the threat of poverty that can arise with sudden illness or redundancy.

Poverty is thus a condition that ultimately threatens a majority of the population. The attempt to define a 'poverty line' merely recognises that there are different standards of living amongst them: that there are gradations in income between those in different jobs, as also between those who have work and those who don't.

The shift from seeing poverty as the condition of existence of a working class to defining it as a certain level of income – a shift that was largely attributable to the rise of the social sciences at the end of the nineteenth century – has been a development of profound political significance. It has, at one level, weakened Senior's 'unfortunate' contrast between rich and poor, and perhaps more importantly served to portray 'the poor' as a specific and peculiar group separate from the rest of society, and with little by way of common links and interests between them. Together with the stigma that has equally and over a similar period been attached to being poor, this has served to isolate the poorest of the working class from the remainder, and at its worst provided many of the latter with a negative reference point from which they have sought to distance themselves.

It is through such processes that the poor become isolated, for poverty is much more than an inadequate level of income. To be poor is often also to be powerless, to be at the whim of officials and state agencies, and to be dependent upon their decisions for the most basic necessities of life. It is to have no control over the future, to be unable to plan for more than the next week or day. Living in poverty leaves no room for error, and for many means only the most monotonous existence. For some it means even less than that: it means having to make decisions between spending what little money there is either on heating or on food, often in the full knowledge that such decisions mean falling behind into greater debt. It also means being unable to enjoy the normal social life of other people – the holidays, the birthday parties or having a meal out – that others take for granted as part of their standard of living. Yet to be poor does not mean to be immune from such needs and expectations. As John Hobson argued at the end of the nineteenth century:

The difference between felt wants and the power to satisfy them is genuine destitution, and the real danger of poverty in any state is measured by its amount... This is the peculiar danger of our recent civilisation. The modern means of popular education, our school system, the spread of cheap reading, our railways, the growth of facile communications of every kind, and, most potent of all, the experience of new sensations and the stimulation of new ideas provided by city life, have constantly and rapidly enlarged the scope of desires of the poorer classes ... more rapidly than the increase in the means of satisfaction.

(Hobson 1896:498)

This generation of dissatisfaction – 'a universal, perpetual never-satisfied desire for something better than anything that is ever realised' (Rea 1912:10) – is one of the fundamental mechanisms that capitalism has generated in order to maintain its process of accumulation and, in an increasingly affluent society, to reinforce the incentive to work. The mass production of consumer goods has brought with it an unending attempt to persuade people to consume more and more. Daily the television adverts, the newspapers, magazines and hoardings attempt to persuade us that we need a new washing machine or car: we are presented with life-styles based on the consumption of goods and services that are portrayed as normal and achievable, yet which for a majority of the population remain always out of reach. People are offered credit in unending quantities to help them get there – by the end of 1985 total personal debt amounted to 85 per cent of income with repayments accounting for 10 per cent of all expenditure – only to find that they have to work even harder to pay off the debt on last year's now outdated model.

In the meantime the number of people pushed to the margin of economic and social life continues to grow relentlessly, as an increasingly wider gap opens up between rich and poor. In 1984, for example, the average household income of the poorest twenty per cent of the population stood at £47 per week: just over one-tenth of the £417 per week enjoyed by the richest twenty per cent. In a poll commissioned by the *Sunday Times*, ten million people in Britain reported that they could not afford even a week's holiday; seven million admitted that they had had to go without food at least once in the previous twelve months; and over three million were found to be living in damp houses that they could not afford to heat. Such poverty in the midst of plenty is no accident; it is not the result of shortage and scarcity; it is not a residual and declining problem, but one of massive and growing proportions. It is a problem whose implications and consequences may yet prove explosive.

two

THE RELIEF OF POVERTY

The battle of ideas; the 1834 Poor Law Report; a moral economy; the right to relief; the laws of nature; the principle of less eligibility; the problem of centralisation; the interventionist state.

> Those that get their living by their daily labour...have
> nothing to stir them up to be serviceable but their wants,
> which it is prudence to relieve, but folly to cure.
> (Bernard de Mandeville 'The Fable of the Bees'. Cited Karl
> Marx *Capital* Vol. I:576)

The creation of a working class was the product of a long historical development. By the time of the industrial revolution in Britain such a class had been brought into existence. But a working class has constantly to be re-created as a *working* class. There is nothing 'natural' or inevitable about wage labour, although much effort has gone into making it appear as such. As Marx argued:

> Nature does not produce on the one side owners of money or
> commodities, and on the other men possessing nothing but
> their labour power. This relation has no natural basis.... It is
> clearly the result of a past historical development, the product
> of many economic revolutions, of the extinction of a whole
> series of older forms of social organisation.
> (Marx 1974:166)

On the contrary, the inequalities and suffering it gives rise to, the harsh realities that many people face in earning a living, its consequences in terms of poverty and unemployment, and the continuing contrast between rich and poor, constantly poses capitalism with problems of questioning, resistance and opposition.

The maintenance of capitalism has thus required more than just the physical maintenance and reproduction of a working class; it has required a series of incentives and punishments. It has required also the creation of specific ideologies – ideologies, for example, about the inevitability of and responsibility for poverty, about the 'natural' role and responsibilities of women or about work and a work ethic. The weight of centuries and, above all, the very necessity created by poverty has been 'the most potent mechanism for maintaining the incentive to work. As J. Townsend put it somewhat bluntly in his 'Dissertation on the Poor Laws' in 1786:

> There must be a degree of pressure, and that which is attended with the least violence will be the best. When hunger is either felt or feared, the desire of obtaining bread will quietly dispose the mind to undergo the greatest hardships, and will sweeten the severest labours.
>
> (Cited Poynter 1969:xvi)

Almost two hundred years later, the Supplementary Benefits Commission in its evidence to the Committee on Abuse of Social Security Benefits was to be almost equally as forthright:

> There has to be a certain amount of pressure on claimants to find work and stay in it, and it is a matter of hard fact that this involves letting it be known that state money is not there for the asking for anyone who is able to work but unwilling to do so.
>
> (Report 1973:109)

Hunger, however, is rather a blunt weapon. It has been, and is, frequently used, but it is a weapon that has to be used selectively. The sheer scale of poverty, and the destitution that faces those who, however great or harsh the incentives, cannot whether through old age, sickness or unemployment find work has meant that some form of relief against poverty has had to be provided in order to prevent poverty breaking out into open rebellion.

There is, however, more than just political realism involved in the relief of poverty. Certainly it would be unthinkable for any government of an advanced capitalist society to abolish all forms of relief. But even from the time of the industrial revolution it has been recognised that the relief of poverty also carries with it a powerful means of manipulation and control, much more subtle, safer and effective than the weapon of hunger. As Sir George Nicholls, one of the three Commissioners appointed to implement the new Poor Law after 1834 reported, at first:

> we contemplated the workhouse as little more than an instrument of economy... It was not until the results began to be developed that the full consequences of the *mitigated kind of necessity* imposed on the working classes by a well regulated workhouse were understood and appreciated. We saw then that it compelled them, *bred* them to be industrious, sober, provident, careful of themselves, of their parents and children.
>
> (Cited Poynter 1969:315)

It is in the ways in which poverty is relieved – in the conditions on which, to whom, and in the manner in which relief is granted – that the state has built up a powerful weapon to influence social relationships: to maintain the incentive to work, to favour or discourage particular forms of family life, to reinforce the economic dependence of women, or to influence and mould perceptions of poverty.

The battle of ideas

The rise of industrial capitalism in Britain depended, as we have seen, on the prior development of capitalist relations of wage labour in agriculture. The appearance of an industrial bourgeoisie, however, was not to be without conflict. The owners of the new factories and mills faced a society that was predominantly rural, that had its own specific set of social relationships and ideologies, and that was governed by a class that wished to hold on to its own position of influence and power.

When the Civil War had broken the last political stronghold of the feudal ruling class, political power had passed to an amalgam of landed gentry and merchants. As E.P. Thompson has described it:

The main beneficiaries were those vigorous agrarian capitalists, the gentry. But this does not mean that the governing
institutions represented, in an unqualified manner, the gentry
as a 'ruling class'. At a local level (the magistracy) they did so in
an astonishingly naked manner. At a national level...a
distance opened up between the majority of the middle and
lesser gentry and certain agrarian magnates, privileged merchant capitalists, and their hangers-on, who manipulated the
organs of State in their own interest. Nor was this a simple
'class' tension...certain magnates only were on the 'inside',
and influence swung according to factional politics... It
should be seen less as government by an aristocracy...than as
a parasitism... It was nothing but itself. A unique formation.
Old Corruption.

(Thompson 1965:322)

While industrialisation gave the new industrial bourgeoisie great
economic power, it did not give them a commensurate political
power. This they had to fight for. Such battles, however, are not
only fought with swords: ideas can themselves be a potent,
material force, giving an identity and cohesion to a scattered
group of individuals, and used as a weapon against existing ideas
and the practices they represent. For the rising industrial
bourgeoisie, one such set of ideas was formed in the philosophy
of political economy.

Political economy – the 'science of wealth' – was both an
attempt to understand the workings of a capitalist economy and
to formulate the 'laws' by which it operated, and a means of
intellectual propaganda to wage a war on Old Corruption. The
writings of Adam Smith and others stressed production, rather
than simply the ownership of land, as the source of wealth. They
attacked aristocratic power and privilege as parasitic, and, since
bourgeois political economy stressed a common identity and
interest between the 'productive classes' of workers and
employers, held the taxation required to support Old Corruption
to be responsible for the poverty of the masses.

Armed with such a theory the industrial bourgeoisie set about
to whip up working class discontent, and to ride it in a battle
against the aristocracy for political reform. The example of the
French revolution added a further impetus to the movement, and
an equally repressive response from the government, which

imprisoned radical working class leaders, prohibited trade union organisation, placed a prohibitive tax on working class newspapers, and, as at Peterloo, met even peaceful protest with force. At the same time, while opposition grew, the working class movement began also to question the claims of political economy:

> For twenty years... working class theorists had recognised that there was a gap between what the labourer produced and what his wage would buy, and in turn taxation, upper class parasites, the theft of land, and competition were held to account for it. Any more devastating critique was inhibited because... [of the inclusion of] the manufacturers among the productive classes.
>
> (Hollis 1970:217)

Increasingly however it was recognised that it was not merely the aristocracy who oppressed the working class, but that a far greater toll was taken in the process of capitalist production itself. As one working class newspaper saw it:

> Enormous taxation is no doubt an evil; but it is only one of a number of evils, many of them equally oppressive as taxation... RENTS and TITHES and INTEREST of money, and tolls, and above all, of the *profits realised on capital*, which is greater than all the other burdens put together.
>
> (Cited Hollis 1973:15)

Through the closing years of the 1820s, the bourgeoisie struggled to maintain control of working class discontent and direct it towards the demand for parliamentary reform. In 1830, in the midst of widespread campaigns and demonstrations throughout the country, violent unrest broke out in the agricultural counties of the south: 'several counties were in a state bordering on insurrection' (Hammond 1913:44). The Tory government under the Duke of Wellington resigned, to be replaced by the Whigs, 'the aristocratic representatives of the bourgeoisie' (Marx and Engels 1975:109). As Lord Grey, its leader, argued:

> With regard to this war... I can only promise that the state of the country shall be made the object of our immediate attention... To relieve the distress which now so unhappily

exists in different parts will be the first and most anxious end of our deliberations; but I here declare...that it is my determined resolution, wherever outrages are perpetuated, or excesses committed, to suppress them with severity and vigour. (Cheers).

(Cited Hollis 1973:120)

For the latter part, Grey was true to his word: Special Commissions were appointed to investigate the riots – nine people were hanged, four hundred and fifty-seven people transported, and over four hundred imprisoned (Hammond 1913:308). As for the promise to relieve the distress which had occasioned the revolts, further action was to wait for nearly two years. In the meantime a more urgent task awaited the government which, in Grey's words, was 'to associate the middle with the higher order of society in the love and support of the institutions and government of the country' (cited Thompson 1974:899). In 1832, after a series of setbacks and crises in which, according to E.P. Thompson, 'England was within an ace of a revolution which, once commenced, might well have prefigured, in its radicalisation, the revolutions of 1848 and the Paris Commune' (op cit:898), Grey succeeded in pushing a Reform Bill through Parliament which gave the vote to the new industrial bourgeoisie. Two months before the Reform Act was passed he kept his earlier promise by appointing a Royal Commission to investigate the state of the Poor Law.

The 1834 Poor Law Report

The Report of the Poor Law Commission was published in 1834; within six months its principal recommendations had begun to be put into effect, giving rise to a national supervision of poor relief and a set of principles in its administration which have ever since continued to form the basis of Britain's system of social security provision.

The writing of the Report, as well as the greater part of the work of the Commission itself, was undertaken by two men: Nassau Senior, Professor of Political Economy at Oxford, and Edwin Chadwick, student of the philosopher and political economist Jeremy Bentham, and in his own right a leading authority on social reform (see Finer 1952; Levy 1970; Bowley 1949). Both men were part of a small but influential group of what could be called early major civil servants. This group, including also such people as the factory inspector Leonard Horner and the educationalist Sir James Kay-Shuttleworth were together to establish during the course of the nineteenth century the systems of poor relief, public education, health, housing and factory legislation that form the core of contemporary social policy. In this respect they were also the architects of the modern state, creating not only its underlying policies and principles but also the political structures and institutions upon and through which the state's power was itself built and extended.

The Poor Law Commission, of which there were nine members including Chadwick and Senior, itself appointed twenty-six unpaid Assistant Commissioners who were to visit and report on some one-fifth of the existing Poor Law parishes. Like most subsequent investigations of poverty or social security – the surveys, for example, of Booth and Rowntree at the end of the nineteenth century, the Beveridge Report of 1942, or the Committee on Abuse of Social Security Benefits chaired by the merchant banker Sir Henry Fisher in 1973 – the inquiry was undertaken by men, and by men of property. The experiences and needs of women, who then as now were the majority of recipients of relief, or of the poor in general, were not given a voice.

Although the Report of 1834 was to base its arguments on evidence submitted by the Assistant Commissioners, its purpose had already been well defined beforehand. This purpose was spelt out to the Assistant Commissioners before they commenced their work:

> There are two general enquiries to which each specific enquiry may be made subservient. One is the great question how far the law which throws on the owners of property the duty of providing the subsistence and superintending the conduct of the poor, has really effected its object; how far the proprietors of land and capital appear to have had the power and the will to create, or increase, or render secure the prosperity and morality of those who live by the wages of labour.
>
> ('Instructions From the Central Board of Poor Law
> Commissioners to Assistant Commissioners'.
> Reprinted in Extracts . . . 1837:425)

The 'morality' of the working class was a central concern of nineteenth-century political economists, just as it has, in differing forms, continued to be a major preoccupation of state policy. Political economy (at least in its more sophisticated forms) recognised that production was not only an economic but also a social and political process: that it depended upon the existence and maintenance of a certain set of social relationships between different classes. In other words, it recognised that capitalism was inevitably a political as well as an economic system. Moreover, it understood that the construction of this social order could not safely be left to the blind operation of market forces:

> The social body cannot be constructed like a machine, on abstract principles which merely include physical motions and their numerical results in the production of wealth ... Political economy, though its object be to ascertain the means of increasing the wealth of nations, cannot accomplish its designs without at the same time regarding the cultivation of religion and morality.
>
> (Kay-Shuttleworth 1832:64)

Kay-Shuttleworth and the other major civil servants recognised, in a way that later economists seem often to have forgotten, that labour, although bought and sold under capitalism, is not like other commodities: that it has feelings and a capacity to think, and that 'the folly which neglects them is allied to madness' (ibid: 112). The successful exploitation of this commodity therefore required the cultivation of morality – of certain attitudes, behaviour and beliefs – amongst the working class, which were as essential to the economic success of capitalism as they were to its political stability. Where the 'right' kind of behaviour or attitude was lacking, this had to be transformed by the creation of new institutions and practices, which could ultimately only be done effectively by the state. This then was the task which the early civil servants set themselves: to create, through the various mechanisms of poor relief, state education, health, housing or factory legislation, the necessary social, economic and political relations on which the stability of capitalism would depend.

In the view of the Commissioners, perhaps the greatest obstacle to securing the appropriate morality of the working class was the existing system of poor relief: a system which had developed largely in response to the needs of a rural agrarian economy and its political stability, and which they now argued to be the cause of a widespread 'demoralisation' of the working class that had resulted in the growing social and political conflict between workers and their employers which dominated the opening decades of the nineteenth century. As their Instructions to their Assistant Commissioners went on to point out:

It has been maintained that it is the natural tendency of public relief . . . to become a substitute, and a very bad substitute . . . for industry and forethought on the part of the poor . . . If the progress of the evils . . . may be traced in the diminished cultivation and value of the land; the diminution of industry, forethought, and natural affection amongst the labourers; the conversion of wages from a matter of contract to a matter of right . . . in the accelerated increase of every form of profligacy, in fires, riots, and almost treasonable robbery and devastation; if such be the representation which the Commissioners have to make to His Majesty, they cannot append to it a suggestion of mere palliative amendments.

(Extracts 1837:425)

This, then, was the brief upon which one of the most significant state inquiries in the history of the welfare state was to be undertaken: the falling value of land, increasing unemployment and destitution, and rising class conflict and discontent were to be blamed not on the uneven development and violent fluctuations of an emerging industrial economy, nor on the depressed state of agriculture and its consequent underemployment and poverty, but on the practice and even the very existence of the system of poor relief.

A moral economy

The Commissioners could not have been unaware that they were writing their Report firstly for a Parliament of landowners. Although the 1832 Reform Act had carefully extended the franchise to the new industrial bourgeoisie, Parliament in effect remained dominated by a landowning aristocracy. The Commissioners thus knew that whatever reforms were proposed would have to depend upon their support; 'a good administration of the Poor Laws', they argued, 'is the landlord's interest' (Report 1834:151).

This administration they found to be corrupt and defective. Within each of the 15,000 parishes in England and Wales, primary responsibility rested with the local Vestry – a collection of elected or self-appointed property-owners and ratepayers responsible, amongst other things, for the appointment of an Overseer and the collection of the poor rate. According to the Commission:

> They form the most irresponsible bodies that were ever entrusted with the performance of public duties, or the distribution of public money ... Each vestryman, so far as he is an immediate employer of labour, is interested in keeping down the rate of wages, and in throwing part of their payment on others ... if he is the owner of cottages, he endeavours to get their rent paid by the parish; if he keeps a shop, he struggles to get allowances for his customers or debtors ...
>
> (Report 1834:192)

Similarly the position of Overseer of the Poor – an unpaid post rotated annually or quarterly amongst the ratepayers – was seen as open to abuse and fraud. The Overseer was often 'an uneducated man ...':

> the persons appointed are in general farmers in county places, and shopkeepers or manufacturers in towns ... If, as an immediate employer of labour, he is interested in keeping down its price, he may gain, or think that he gains, more by the reduction of wages than he loses by the rise of rates.
>
> (Report 1834:181)

The greatest force of its criticism of the administration of relief, however, was directed not at corruption but at the central role played by the Justices of the Peace. Created originally by the feudal monarchy in its battle for national control over local interests, the Justices had come to assume a position of ultimate authority over a number of parishes, with power to over-rule the decisions of vestries and overseers. It was this power that, according to one Assistant Commissioner, was 'a principal cause of the high rates', since the Justices of the Peace were frequently the targets for the complaints and demands of the poor, and 'a gentleman of property, without experience in the employment of labour, is easily imposed upon by their false representations' (Report 1834:226).

As 'gentlemen of property', rather than employers of labour, the magistrates did indeed exist in a different relationship to the poor: a relationship which the Commissioners fully recognised and saw as one of the major obstacles to change. It was a relationship which, in general, embodied an older ideology of paternalism: an ideology of a stable and hierarchical rural order which, while it argued that the poor were to remain in their place, offered them in return the care and protection of the rich – they 'considered themselves protectors of the poor' (Report 1834:229). Part of this ideology was spelt out in more detail by the Justice of the Peace for Shoreditch:

> I do not think that the character of the pauper, if he is in distress, can be taken into consideration; for the Poor Laws were not established as a reward for good conduct, but as a provision for the person in immediate distress, and a person just discharged from the house of correction, or a prostitute, is as much entitled to relief as the most respectable pauper in the parish.
>
> (Report 1834:235)

It was, however, precisely as an instrument of moralisation – as a reward for good behaviour or, more often, as a punishment for bad – that the authors of the Report wished to see the Poor Law used, and the ideology of the Justices of the Peace rankled most strongly with them:

> Great evils arise from their interference ... In the first place, the very mode in which their jurisdiction is enforced seems intended to destroy all vigilance and economy on the part of those who administer relief, and all sense of shame and degradation on those who receive it.
>
> (Report 1834:220)

The Commissioners were not unaware of the strength of this ideology, of notions of a 'moral economy' and of the right to relief, nor of its importance in the political structure of the rural economy and its social order. This 'moral economy' – halfway in the transition from feudalism to capitalism – laid claim to the rights of the poor, and stressed the obligations of the rich towards them (see Thompson 1971). Moreover, rooted as it was in a hierarchical and traditional rural order, it in many ways opposed the development of an industrial capitalism, which it saw as threatening the fragility of social order by its greed for accumulation and its treatment of workers simply as commodities.

This moral economy had been one of the points around which the emerging working class movement was able to create an alliance with certain aristocratic elements within the ruling class in their resistance to the factory system; it was also to provide a basis for opposition to the implementation of the 'new' Poor Law after 1834, and was still to find a pale echo in the so-called 'wets' of the Conservative Party that felt the withering scorn of Thatcherism in the 1980s. Enshrined in legislation, in the paternalistic ideology of a landowning aristocracy, but above all in popular tradition and belief that clung to and fought to maintain the notion of the right of the poor to relief and to be treated decently, it had nevertheless been increasingly eroded under the growing impact of market forces, and just as fiercely reasserted in a series of forms of popular direct action throughout the eighteenth and early nineteenth centuries (see Thompson 1971).

Whilst the Poor Law Commissioners sought to suggest to their investigating Assistants that the activities of the Justices might be found to stem from corruption and self-interest (see Extracts 1837:420), they were ultimately forced to concede that:

> The magistrates have exercised the powers delegated to them by the Poor Laws – not wisely, indeed, or beneficially, but still with benevolent and honest intentions, and that the mischief that they have done was not the result of self-interest or partiality, or timidity, or negligence, but was, in part, *the necessary consequence of their social position.*
>
> (Report 1834:290. Emphasis added)

It was the social position of the magistracy within a rural agrarian economy and its social relations which guided their actions. But this economy was increasingly giving way to an urban and industrial one. Just as the authors of the Report were to see their task as establishing the social relations and institutions appropriate to this new order, so it was inevitable that they would need to challenge the authority, cohesion and power of the magistrates. As Nassau Senior remarked privately in a letter to Lord Brougham in 1832:

> The means of obtaining popularity and exerting influence which the present system gives to the magistrates seems to be, with most of them, superior to any other consideration. They appear, also, from their replies, to be actuated by an *esprit de corps* more intense than that of any other class of functionaries ... I have no hope of real improvement while their power of interference remains undiminished and no hope that they will voluntarily surrender a single particle of it.
>
> (Cited Levy 1970:249)

The right to relief

While the Report thus gave considerable space to criticism of the existing structure and administration of the Poor Law, its greatest attention was focused on the effects of this administration on the poor and the working class itself. Thus while it decried petty corruption, the rising cost of poor relief, and the declining value and rent of land, it considered that:

> The severest sufferers are those for whose benefit the system is supposed to have been introduced, and to be perpetuated, the labourers and their families ... those that have become callous to their own degradation, who value parish support as their privilege, and demand it as their right.
>
> (Report 1834:167)

That the poor considered they had a right to relief was, as we have seen, an established part of the social tradition and structure of pre-industrial capitalism. According to one of the many radical working class newspapers that flourished at the beginning of the nineteenth century:

> The right of these people to poor relief is of more than two centuries standing. It was given them in exchange for their share of the church property, of which the Reformation despoiled them. It was their 'vested interest' in the most enlarged sense of those words, for it was not only guaranteed

by the law of the land, but also by those of justice, humanity
and sound religion.

(The Poor Man's Guardian 18/10/1834)

Or as one of the Assistant Commissioners saw it:

> The poor rate is considered by the lower order as a fund in
> which they have an absolute property, and they do not scruple
> at artifice, violence or fraud to establish their claim to it. This
> feeling contributes more than any other cause to the general
> demoralisation which prevails in the lower ranks of society.
>
> (Report 1834:145)

The demand for the right to work or the right to relief is not a
new one. Ever since the advent of capitalism created a working
class dependent on the sale of its labour-power, workers have
demanded the right either to be allowed to work or, failing that,
to be provided with an adequate standard of living. It was this
morality that the Poor Law Commission regarded as the most
fundamental obstacle to be overcome, for to guarantee a right to
work or relief undermined the discipline of insecurity on which a
wage labour market depended. According to political economy,
responsibility for securing employment had to be laid at the feet
not of employers or of the state but of individual workers
themselves:

> We deplore the misconception [sic] of the labourers in thinking
> that wages are not a matter of contract but of right; that any
> diminution of their comforts . . . is an evil to be remedied, not
> by themselves, but by the magistrates; not an error, or even a
> misfortune, but an injustice.
>
> (Report 1834:325)

Moreover, as the Report recognised, the very existence of
claims of a right to work or relief was a focal point of working
class discontent and organisation: 'the tribunal which enforces it
sits, not at the petty sessions, but at the beer shop; it compels
obedience, not by distress and summons, but by violence and
conflagration' (Report 1834:182). Or as Senior himself recognised
in 1832, following the widespread rural riots and insurrections of
two years earlier:

> The riots, and still more the fires, of 1830 were a practical

lesson on the rights of the poor and the means of enforcing them, the fruits of which are far from being exhausted ... Wages and allowances were raised; the parish pay was increased ... and for a time it seemed to be admitted that landlords, tithe owners and farmers are mere trustees for the labourers, and entitled only to the surplus (if any) after the labourers have received the wages and relief which they may think proper to require. The immediate terror has passed off; some of the extravagant rates of wages and allowances have been reduced; but the labourers have not forgotten *what* were the rights they then established, nor the overseers or magistrates *how* they were established.

(Cited Levy 1970:249)

To take issue with the notion of a right to relief was, therefore, for the Commissioners an urgent task not only of principle but of political necessity.

The 'laws of nature'

The objections raised by the Poor Law Commission against the existing system of poor relief went far beyond issues of corruption to invoke fundamental principles concerning the relief of poverty in a capitalist society. The experience of the industrial revolution, and the rise of the 'science' of political economy as an attempt to understand the mechanisms by which capitalism operated, created the opportunity for just such an assessment. In doing so, political economy was to take the social relations and requirements of capitalist production and proclaim them as the product of natural and immutable laws governing human behaviour.

According to many political economists, the provision of relief against poverty was, at best, an irrelevant relic from a bygone era. It was seen as a system that had developed to provide stability through the decline of feudalism – 'an attempt to restore the expiring system of slavery' (Senior 1865:47) – and that had continued as a means of securing the specific social relations of a hierarchical and agrarian society. But that society was now itself in dissolution, rapidly being replaced by an urban and industrial one. As Sir James Kay-Shuttleworth, who was later to be the key civil servant in the creation of a national system of state education, argued:

The poor-laws as at present administered retain all the evils of
the gross and indiscriminate bounty of ancient monasteries...
The custom is not now demanded as the prop of any
superstition; nor is it fit that institutions, well calculated to
assuage the miseries which feudalism inflicted on its unemployed and unhappy serfs, should be allowed to perpetuate
indigence, improvidence, idleness and vice in a commercial
community. The artificial structure of society, in providing
security against existing evils, has too frequently neglected
the remote moral influence of its arrangements on the
community... The unlimited extension of benefits has a
direct tendency to encourage among the poor apathy concerning present exigencies, and the neglect of a provision for
the contingencies of the future.

(Kay-Shuttleworth 1832:45)

The 'artificial structure' of poor relief had thus to be removed; its
very existence, as the authors of the Report were to argue, was
itself the principal cause of the great 'demoralisation' of the
labouring population:

The labourer feels that the existing system, though it gives
him low wages, always gives him easy work. It gives him also,
strange as it may appear [sic], what he values more, a sort of
independence. He need not bestir himself to please his master;
he need not put any restraint on his temper; he need not ask
relief as a favour. He has all the slave's security for subsistence
without his liability to punishment.

(Report 1834:132)

Such phraseology, moreover, was not misplaced. According to
political economy, wage labour was freedom. It is, as we have
seen earlier, a peculiar kind of 'freedom'. For while at a
philosophical level it proclaims an end to servitude, with everyone
equal and free to make their own individual bargain in the market
place, in reality those dependent on wage labour have no choice
but to sell their labour. It was this 'freedom' of workers to sell
their labour on the market, as well as to be responsible for their
failure to do so, that the authors of the Report wished to
establish. Thus according to Senior:

The Poor Laws ultimately succeeded in many districts in

giving to the labourer and his family the security of servitude.
They succeeded in relieving him and those who, in a real state
of freedom would have been dependent on him, from many of
the penalties imposed by nature on idleness, improvidence and
misconduct . . . Before the Poor Law Amendment Act, nothing
but the power of arbitrary punishment was wanting in the
pauperised parishes to complete a system of praedial slavery.
(Senior 1865:12)

By 1834 the abolition of this 'artificial' structure of relief was
seen, at least by political economists, not only as freedom, but as
'natural': the achievement of capitalism, as well as the task of
political economy, was to free society of those unnecessary and
unnatural constraints on the operation of the market economy;
such an economy alone reflected the true state of human nature:
a human nature that was competitive, self-seeking and individualised, in which people as individuals (or, more properly, as
families) had the responsibility to make their own fortunes or
bear their own troubles:

It appears to the pauper that the Government has undertaken
to repeal, in his favour, the ordinary laws of nature; to enact
that the children shall not suffer for the misconduct of their
parents – the wife for that of the husband, or the husband for
that of the wife. In short, that the penalty which, after all,
must be paid by someone for improvidence and idleness, is to
fall not on the guilty person and his family, but on the
proprietors of the land and houses encumbered by his
settlement.

(Report 1834:135)

The 'laws' of political economy and the 'laws' of nature were thus
to be fused in the 1834 Poor Law Amendment Act.

The principle of less eligibility

The Poor Law Amendment Act was a device designed to give
effect to the principal recommendations of the Report:

It may be assumed that in the administration of relief the
public is warranted in imposing such conditions on the
individual relieved as are conducive to the benefit either of the

individual himself, or of the country at large, at whose expense he is relieved.

(Report 1834: 335)

Of these:

The first and most essential of all conditions... is that his situation on the whole shall not be made really or apparently so eligible as the situation of the independent labourer of the lowest class.

(ibid)

This principle of less eligibility – the principle that relief by the state should always be less attractive than independent wage labour – has ever since been at the heart of the system of social security. The Supplementary Benefits Commission, for example, defined it in relation to the 'wage stop' – a device used until the early 1970s for limiting the benefit paid to unemployed claimants to a level below that which they would normally receive in work, regardless of need:

The principle is that it would be unfair [sic] to the man who was working but earning less than the supplementary benefit level if his counterpart who was unemployed received a higher income.

(Handbook 1971)

The principle of making conditions of relief less attractive than the lowest-paid work was an obvious reflection of the need to maintain poverty as an incentive to work. In practice, however, to make relief less eligible than the lowest-paid work is much more difficult, since it is a permanent feature of capitalism that a number – sometimes more, sometimes less, but always a significant proportion – of those in full-time work themselves earn wages only just on or even below subsistence level. To reduce levels of relief below that of the wages paid to the lowest-paid workers is therefore to risk malnutrition and even starvation. From the point of view of the state, this problem is even further complicated by the fact that the wage system takes no account of the individual family commitments of workers; hence again to provide even subsistence relief for those with an above average number of dependants may often be to exceed what they could obtain on the labour market.

For the Poor Law Report, the solution to the dilemma was to lie in part in the way it had talked of making relief 'not really or apparently so eligible': for if the level of relief could not be made worse than wage labour in reality, then it could be made apparently so. It could be subject to a humiliation and a stigma that would mark it off as far worse than a life of 'independence'. As Sir George Nicholls, one of the three Commissioners appointed in 1834 to implement the new Act, put it:

> I wish to see the Poor House looked to with dread by the labouring classes, and the reproach for being an inmate of it extend down from father to son ... For without this, where is the needful stimulus to industry?
>
> (Cited Poynter 1969:314)

For this purpose the institution of the Workhouse was proposed as both the ultimate 'test' of destitution – since, or so the argument went, only the truly destitute would be prepared to submit themselves to its regime – and as the means to maintain and reinforce the stigma of pauperism. Workhouses were not new, and had been in existence as early as the seventeenth century, when they had been set up as places of employment for the able-bodied poor. Now they were to be turned into places of discipline and terror; families were to be divided, husbands from wives and parents from children; all would be subject to a strict and monotonous regime, dressed in a pauper's uniform, and made to perform tasks such as stone-breaking or unpicking tarred rope. According to one Assistant Commissioner, the effect of such a regime was transformatory:

> New life, new energy is infused into the constitution of the pauper; he is like one aroused from sleep; his relations with all his neighbours, high and low, is transformed; he surveys his former employers with new eyes. He begs a job.
>
> (Report 1834:358)

People still beg jobs, and although the workhouse has disappeared as an instrument of social policy, the principle of less eligibility in relief and the stigma attached to it remains. The modern-day social security office, with its wire meshes and glass screens, its chairs bolted to the floor, its interminable queues and waiting and its persistent treatment of claimants as second-class citizens continues to make the point that the experience of being a claimant is as important a deterrent as the low levels of benefit offered.

The problem of centralisation

The proposals of the Poor Law Commission for the principles by which relief was to be given found little opposition and much support from within the ruling class. What did excite a great deal more opposition was its recommendations for a greater degree of central government control over its administration.

Until this time, the administration of the Poor Law had remained firmly within the control of 15,000 local parishes, each of which, while acting within the framework of national legislation, had the power to decide the level of relief and to whom and on what conditions it would be granted. In the view of the Report, this was a recipe for disaster, not simply in the opportunity it provided for local corruption, but more important-ly in the way it enabled relief to be subjected to political pressure from the poor themselves:

> Whatever may have been the various causes of the agricul-tural riots...the one effect has been to prove that the discretion exercised in the distribution of the Poor's rates can be effected by intimidation.... Under these circumstances, any discretionary power left to the local officers must be a source of suspicion.
>
> (Report 1834:408)

For the Poor Law Commission, therefore, some degree of centralised control was essential. Moreover, only the power of the central state was capable of bringing the desired changes about; it alone was capable of over-riding local vested interests, of overcoming the disabling effects of competition between employers, and pursuing a more long-term and effective strategy. As Marx and Engels argued in *The Communist Manifesto*, 'the executive of the modern state is but a committee for managing the common affairs of the whole of the bourgeoisie'. The import-ance of the state, and of the key civil servants such as Senior or Kay-Shuttleworth within it, is its ability to identify what these common interests are. With a bourgeoisie divided by competition and with its horizons often limited by the pursuit of short-term profitability to the neglect of its longer-term interests and stability, the state plays a crucial role in pulling them into line and pursuing such interests on their behalf. In such a task, of course, care had to be taken not to go too far and lose support. Then, as now, local vested interests remained strong, particular employers were to seek to continue to use the Poor Law to suit the needs of their own particular labour markets (see Digby 1975) and divisions within the ruling class were reflected in distrust of central government control. Whatever the vision and aspirations of those involved in the formation of a national state, they had to tread carefully. As Lord Russell warned Chadwick, 'in the improvement of our institutions . . . we must beware not to lose the co-operation of the country . . . Some faults must be indulged for the sake of carrying improvements in the mass' (cited Richards 1975:115).

While political realism was one reason for ruling out a wholly centralised system of poor relief, another was the fear that 'in time the vigilance and economy, unstimulated by any private interest, would be relaxed; that the workhouses would be allowed to breed an hereditary workhouse population and would cease to be objects of terror' (Report 1834:276). Fears that central government would be unable to exercise sufficiently close control, and that any attempt to establish a national system would be seen as a re-assertion of the right to relief was to delay the creation of a national administration for a hundred years. In the meantime, the 'private interest' of upper and middle class ratepayers was to be retained as a means of securing economy and vigilance, while they were to do so under the direction and guidance of a central board of inspectors.

Under the terms of the 1834 Poor Law Amendment Act, therefore, a Poor Law Commission was established, like many of its successors independent of direct Parliamentary control, to implement the 'new' Poor Law. This Commission was composed of three members, each on a salary of £2,000 a year, with Chadwick as their Secretary. In recognition of the fact that 'difficulty may arise in case any immediate and universal remedy is attempted' (cited Rose 1966:99), the Act gave the Commission the power to decide how, when and where the various reforms were to be put into effect. It also gave the Commission power to form a number of existing parishes into larger Poor Law Unions, to reorganise their administration and to issue Orders and Regulations concerning the granting of relief.

Armed with these powers the Commission set about drawing up the boundaries of the new Poor Law Unions and arranging for the elections of Boards of Guardians, from amongst the local property-owners and ratepayers, who were to form the new basis for Poor Law administration. These Boards were then to appoint salaried officials to administer relief according to the instructions of the Commission. The Justices of the Peace, who previously had exercised ultimate authority through their position in the moral economy and political order, were reduced to ex-officio members of the Board. As Nassau Senior later remarked:

> The Poor Law Amendment Act found the county justices each in his own circle the master of the property of the ratepayers, and of the incomes of the labourers. It left them either excluded from influence in the management of their own parishes, or forced to accept a seat in the Board of Guardians, and to debate and vote among shopkeepers and farmers.
>
> (Cited Levy 1970:87)

This 'domestic revolution' (ibid) in the structure of local government signified an important advance in the creation of the modern state. It was both to lay the foundations for a more uniform national system of relief as well as to mark a major step in what was to prove to be a growing conflict between local and central government that has continued to the present day and that has led to an increasing centralisation of political and administrative power. This growing centralisation of government has been the product of a series of conflicts and divisions within the ruling class. It has also, as we shall see later, been a response to the demands of the working class and labour movement for a greater say in the running of public affairs.

The interventionist state

Much has been made by historians of the 'new' Poor Law, and still more has been written about the nature of the state in the nineteenth century – about whether its policies were guided by the principle of *laissez-faire* or of intervention, and if it was interventionist whether this was the product of humanitarianism, of a growing 'public conscience' and awareness of poverty, or the result of 'spontaneous developments in administration' (Cromwell 1966).

Few historians would now assert, as many once did, that the activities of the state during the middle part of the nineteenth century represented a policy of complete *laissez-faire*: that it sought only to clear the ring, to remove obsolete and artificial obstructions and to allow for the untramelled pursuit of individual interests. Indeed it is now recognised that during this period, through factory legislation, sanitary legislation, education, public health measures, and a wide and increasing array of control, inspection and regulation, both the extent and degree to which the state intervened in social and economic life grew enormously, establishing the foundations for the further extension of state activity during the course of the twentieth century.

Curiously, however, the 1834 Poor Law Amendment Act, with its creation of a central controlling Commission, its reorganisation of the local political structures of the country, and its attempt to introduce a national and uniform system of Poor Law administration, has rarely been seen as part of this process. On the contrary, and with few exceptions, the 1834 Poor Law has been seen as the 'ultimate expression' (Mencher 1961:22) of *laissez-faire*; not as part of the process by which a centralised state was built up and the powers of government extended, but its very opposite:

> The welfare state did not have its origin in that repressive system of social police; it is to be found rather in the thinking and in the policies of those who repudiated the paralysing fatalities of less eligibility and the Malthusian political economy from which they sprang.
>
> (McGregor 1957:34)

Consequently the 1834 Poor Law is seen as a negative starting-point for the development of social policy and social reform, for health and factory legislation, schools and medical inspectors and for future developments in social security and poor relief which, according to one social policy writer, form 'a counter-attack against the principles of 1834, and the social and economic doctrines represented by those principles' (Pinker 1973:50).

The problem with such an analysis, that sees a sharp contrast between the 1834 Poor Law and the subsequent development of the welfare state, is that it misunderstands and misrepresents the nature of both. The expansion of welfare provision, as many claimants would testify, has not undermined the principle of less eligibility, while the social and economic doctrines that underlay the Poor Law, far from being repudiated by state intervention, themselves demanded state intervention.

As an ideology, *laissez-faire* argued that the only proper role for the state was the removal of those artificial barriers that obstruct the natural operation of the market. It was a demand that had been raised in opposition to the paternalist control of prices and markets, and that also was used against what were seen as the restrictive practices and ideologies of the 'old' Poor Law in pursuit of a 'free' market in labour. As we have seen, however, such a market does not exist naturally; it did not rise spontaneously to the surface of economic and social life once previous restrictions had been cleared away. On the contrary, the creation and maintenance of a free labour market required the active intervention of the state.

It is only the rhetoric that sees wage labour as natural which allows the 1834 Poor Law to be interpreted as an example of *laissez-faire*. As Pinker would have it, 'those who drafted and administered the Act had no wish to "rule the poor". They wished to direct them, harshly if necessary, along the only true path to freedom' (Pinker 1973: 59). Yet even nineteenth-century political economists recognised that the path to wage labour or the maintenance of a particular form of family life never runs smooth, but requires constant and active reinforcement. As Leonard Horner, one of the main architects of factory legislation, complained:

It quite disgusts me to hear the cold, calculating economists throwing aside all moral considerations, and with entire ignorance of the state of people who work in factories, talk of it being an infringement of principle to interfere with labour.... I could from my experience show the fallacious reasons and *bad* political economy of those very economists who, with their extravagant extensions of the doctrine of

laissez-faire, bring discredit on the science they cultivate.
(Cited McGregor 1957:149)

'Bad' political economy aside, those at the forefront of the building of the modern state recognised the precarious hold of wage labour on the working class and the danger to the stability of capitalism inherent in a system of production which brought them together in such large numbers. As Kay-Shuttleworth put it:

> The operative population constitutes one of the most important elements in society, and when numerically considered, the magnitude of its interests and the extent of its power assume such vast proportions that the folly which neglects them is allied to madness.... When this results not from ignorance it is a crime, and I am not willing to screen from just contempt those who are so blind to the true interests of their own order that they represent the people to be happy and contented.
> (Kay-Shuttleworth 1832:112)

To meet working class discontent – to deal with the great 'demoralisation' of labour – it was not sufficient simply to remove old restrictions; new structures, new practices and new ideologies had to be inserted in their place. A set of institutions had to be created, whether in the form of workhouses, a police force, and later schools and other forms of 'welfare' provision that could create the right sort of morality: the attitudes, beliefs and social relationships that the stability of capitalism required. The state servants who forged these institutions thus took a leading role in educating their own class, in forcing them to recognise the dangers of pauperism, of the short-term pursuit of 'cheap' labour which neglected its moral consequences, and, where necessary, using the power of the state to override particular or local interests in order to do so. Their role was thus to persuade 'the vanguard of the middle class, the industrial capitalists, that the strong state was in their interests' (Richards 1975:102).

To the working class at the time, this was all very obvious: 'The Poor Man's Destruction Bill' wrote *The Poor Man's Guardian* in October 1834, 'is purely and solely the work of the middle or profit-hunting classes'. Or as another of the many working class newspapers explained:

In one respect the New Poor Law has done good. It has helped
to open people's eyes as to who are the real enemies of the
working classes. Previously to the passing of the Reform Bill,
the middle orders were supposed to have some community of
feeling with the labourers. That delusion has passed away. It
barely survived the Irish Coercion Bill, it vanished completely
with the enactment of the Starvation Law.

(Cited Rothstein 1929:99)

The regulation of social life, the creation of a certain set of social
relationships, is itself an economic force. Wage labour is both a
process through which capitalist production takes place and a set
of relationships between groups of people. Political economy, as
its name suggests, recognised this interrelationship. The
creation of the New Poor Law and the establishment of the
principle of less eligibility was thus intended both to discipline
and contain the working class as well as to use the power of the
state to secure the operation of the labour market to the benefit
of capital:

Once adopt the principle that whatever may be the labourer's
condition, the pauper's must still be a degree worse, and that
moment you place the labourer at the utter mercy of the
capitalist – you compel him, in fact, to take whatever wages he
is offered; for if he refuses, he has no other recourse than to go
where he is to be less comfortable still. Twist and turn the
proposition as you may, it inevitably comes to this – its
adoption places the 'independent' labourer at the utter mercy
of his employer.

(*The Poor Man's Guardian* 14.11.1835)

Or as the *Northern Star*, recognising the role played by the
'philosophy' of political economy, put it:

The abolition of the *legal* relief for the unemployed; the denial
of all relief, except on terms that would deter everyone but the
soul-destroyed starving slave from accepting it; the institution of the 'workhouse *test*' with its workhouse dress – its *brand*
of poverty – its classification – its separation of man and wife
and mother and child ... all this was well calculated to make
the labourer *offer his services* for almost any amount of wage,
sooner than subject himself to the cruelties that awaited him if
he applied for aid in his necessity to those facetiously called his

'guardians' . . . And thus 'Philosophy' accomplished its aims. *It got at the wages of labour.*

(Cited Hollis 1973:212)

For over a hundred years while it remained on the statute books, the 1834 Poor Law Amendment Act dominated the experience of poverty in Britain. As an instrument of discipline, as a reminder of the virtues of self-reliance, of women's dependence on marriage and as a means of stigmatising those unable to support themselves, the threat of the workhouse would hang over the heads of generations of the working class elderly, the sick, deserted or unmarried mothers and the unemployed. Certainly, as we shall see, exceptions would be made: the rigour and stigma of relief reduced in certain periods or for certain groups, if for no other reason than political expediency. But the overall message would remain, and has remained despite the repeal of the Poor Law in 1948. It has remained precisely because the principles it established are the principles essential to the relief of poverty in a society where poverty and inequality continue to form the basis for prosperity and wealth.

The 1834 Poor Law was not intended to abolish poverty, since those who framed it understood that poverty is an essential requirement of a capitalist economy. They recognised, however, that in relieving certain of the effects of poverty, the state was possessed of an important instrument of regulation and control. The creation and refinement of this instrument, in the form of the Poor Law, was – like the parallel 'domestic revolution' embarked upon by the Conservative government one hundred and fifty years later – aimed at the creation of a new morality and required the emergence of a strong state. Both Thatcherism and the early nineteenth-century state, however, can claim to be examples of *laissez-faire* only in so far as capitalism, its system of wage labour and its system of values can be claimed to be 'natural' and unproblematic. In reality they are not, but require constant support and intervention. Seen another way, the argument about the state has been a question of who has benefited from state intervention. When – as has occasionally happened – the state is seen to intervene on behalf of the poor, its activity is dismissed as unnatural and destructive; when – as it frequently and most consistently does – it intervenes on behalf of the rich, it is not seen as intervention at all.

part two

UNEMPLOYMENT AND SOCIAL REFORM
1880–1914

three

THE PROBLEM OF UNEMPLOYMENT

A note on self-help; the creation of unemployment; a stirring of revolt; social investigation; the problem of imperialism; the reserve armies of labour; the problem of casual labour; the problem of efficiency; unemployment and the working class.

It looks as if we are in the presence of one of those periodic upheavals in the labour world such as occurred in 1833–34, and from time to time since that date, each succeeding occurrence showing a marked advance in organisation on the part of the workers, and the necessity for a corresponding change of tactics on the part of the employers.

(G. Askwith, 1911. Cited Winter 1974:27)

A great deal can happen over the space of fifty years, even at the relatively slower pace of development of the nineteenth century. In 1834 Britain had still been largely an agricultural country; the majority of the working population were farm labourers, some of whom had moved to the towns and industrial mills and factories in search of work, but it was not to be until 1850 that the balance of the population was to become urban; Parliament had been dominated by a landowning aristocracy, intent on protecting the 'agricultural interest'; and the industrial bourgeoisie, although vociferous and powerful, had yet to bring the whole of the country under its sway. By the 1880s Britain was predominantly an urban industrial nation, producing steel and complex machinery, with a vast network of railways and communication systems, constantly revolutionising the processes of production as the relative power and influence of agriculture declined. It contained a working class that had grown up in the cities, with the influence of Chartism, the experience of factory work and mass trades unionism. From the 1880s the British ruling class was to face the problems of mass unemployment and poverty, imperialism and the threat of socialism. By 1911 there was also to be the motor car, the Suffragette movement, Winston Churchill, Lloyd George, old age pensions and National Insurance.

Between the 1830s and the 1880s lay the massive increase in the productive power of British industry that by the mid-nineteenth century had made Britain 'the workshop of the world'. By the 1840s the leading sectors of the economy – the woollen and textile industries on which the first phase of industrialisation had been based – had already begun to give way to newer industrial forms, and in particular to the production of those capital goods – coal, iron, steel and industrial plant and machinery – on which further expansion and growth was to depend. By the 1840s, for example, Britain produced two-thirds of the world's coal, one half of its iron, five-sevenths of its steel, and consumed two-thirds of the world's total steam power. As a product of this development, Britain also enjoyed some six thousand miles of railway, compared with only seven thousand in the whole of the Americas and thirteen thousand in the rest of Europe. In addition, the total surplus of uninvested capital amounted to some £60 million a year, almost twice the total capital value of the entire cotton industry (Hobsbawm 1974).

In this pattern of growth British capital relied heavily upon the opening up and expansion of international trade and on the colonisation of large parts of the world (including often, as with India, the destruction of its own indigenous forms of production) both to provide a market in which to sell goods and later machinery as the domestic market became satiated, and as a source of cheap raw materials and food to supply its growing industry and to feed its increasingly urban population. Considering themselves at the pinnacle of a mutual and world-wide division of labour, the British bourgeoisie dreamt not only of increasing and unrivalled prosperity, but also of growing internal stability. Reflecting on the defeat and collapse of the anti-Poor Law and Chartist movements some ten years earlier, the *Edinburgh Review* considered that:

> since then time has solved all these problems . . . the enormous increase of our commerce and manufactures . . . have changed the whole complexion of our labouring classes. Penury has

given way to plenty; idleness to employment; disaffection to content.

(Cited Rothstein 1929:184)

The view that the middle half of the nineteenth century was a period of political quiescence when, after the turmoil and conflict of the 1820s and 1830s, the working class finally came to accept capitalism and its 'laws', and sought to improve their position from within rather than challenge it from without, is one that has achieved much currency, and which has been used to try to explain much of subsequent political development in this country. According to one influential commentator on the history of the labour movement, after the defeat of Chartism, the working class:

quickly turned into an apparently docile class. It embraced one species of moderate reformism after another, became a consciously subordinate part of society, and has remained wedded to the narrowest and greyest of bourgeois ideologies in its principal movements.

(Nairn 1972:188)

This apparent decline in working class opposition has been explained as the product of the boom itself: in much the same way that sociologists were to talk of the 'embourgeoisement' largely of white, male factory workers during the 'affluent' years of the 1950s and 1960s, so it has been argued that the growth of industry and engineering during the nineteenth century gave rise to a 'labour aristocracy', again of white male and generally skilled workers with higher wages and greater security who were to see themselves as examples of what could be achieved through the Victorian middle class values of discipline, hard work, abstinence and thrift. It was these workers who established co-operative stores and friendly societies, who it is argued looked down on the unemployed and the unskilled, and who saw the salvation of the working class as lying not in politics but in 'self-help'. In such accounts, the labour aristocracy became 'a specific vehicle of assimilation, whereby bourgeois ideas were refracted down into the working class. The result was not a *naked* imitation of the middle class but a kind of ... *caricature* of bourgeois ultra-respectability' (ibid).

It is this apparent incorporation of the élite of the working class which has been held to account for the subsequent forms of working class politics and organisation in Britain, for the rise of a Labour Party and trade union movement which, rather than transform the structure of society, seeks, in the words of Perry Anderson, 'to defend and improve its own position within a social order accepted as given' (Anderson 1966:72).

As a description of the labour aristocracy during the nineteenth century these accounts are not wholly without foundation; in a period of expansion there was considerable economic and social mobility, and much working class activity and literature was devoted to the promotion of independence and self-reliance. But, just as sociologists in the post-war era were to mistake evidence of consumerism such as eating habits and foreign holidays as signs that car workers and others were becoming 'middle class', so we need also beware of mistaking an appearance for reality. What may appear as the adoption of supposedly bourgeois values such as self-help had a very different origin, meaning and set of implications within a working class culture. Such accounts, moreover, appear unable to explain why it was precisely this 'labour aristocracy' which was to be at the forefront of industrial and political unrest during the first decades of the twentieth century, nor why it was around this group in particular that the fears and activities of social reformers were to be concentrated.

If we are to understand these events, and the full impact and consequences which the re-emergence of mass unemployment was to have for the social and political structure of Britain at the end of the nineteenth century, we will have first for a moment to consider the development of the working class itself.

A note on self-help

The defeat of Chartism after decades of struggle was undoubtedly a blow to what must have been an almost exhausted working class. But the withdrawal from the campaign for universal suffrage was not solely the consequence of defeat. In a public debate on Chartism in 1842, Alex Campbell, the founder of the Glasgow Co-operative movement, put it this way:

> He was well aware that the Chartists supposed that if they had the Charter, then they would be able to send such parties to Parliament as would make those laws which were required for

the good of the people. Now, he must submit that so long as class organisation existed, so long must class legislation exist ... That would equally be the case under a monarchy, or a republic, so long as society was divided into classes. As a proof that a republican form of government was not of itself sufficient to remove the state of anarchy, confusion and want of employment among the poor, he might refer them to America, where they had had more than Chartist institutions for more than half a century, but where they had merely changed the form of government without changing the form of society.

(Cited Youngjohns 1954:26)

It was this recognition that political reform alone was insufficient, that unless 'the form of society' was changed, changes in its political administration would not solve the problems of poverty or unemployment, which lay behind the rejection by a section of the working class of the struggle for Parliamentary reform. Moreover, as the Co-operative movement's journal *The New Moral World* pointed out, without a change in the real relations of power – the power of property and the power to command another person's labour – formal political representation was a 'delusion':

We renounce 'radicalism' – as advocated by political reformers – as a mode of permanently removing the evils of society ... The political suffrage is only one element, and, in our opinion, a comparatively minor one of real equality ... The existence of privileged, wealthy, better-educated, and rival classes in society – the principle of individual competition and individual property – the selling of human labour as a commodity ... are totally incompatible with true democracy. The working classes – the labour sellers, will, under such circumstances, and with the utmost possession of political power they can desire, for ever remain, in reality, the slaves of the privileged, monied, and educated influential classes.

(Cited Youngjohns 1954:32)

Working class self-help was to be a response to this situation: a response which sought to build the strength, resources, and independence of the working class. The development of consumer and producer co-operatives – largely by and within the 'labour aristocracy'–was however only one aspect of a much wider culture and set of organisations and institutions devoted to working class self-help. By far the largest and most organised of these were the Friendly Societies, through which large numbers of working class people developed their own forms of mutual saving and protection against the threats of poverty, unemployment and sickness. By 1872 their membership was estimated at some four million, with a total of eight million beneficiaries, far exceeding the membership of trades unions, and extending beyond the élite of skilled workers to encompass a wide range of workers and their families in a variety of schemes, from the large nationally affiliated organisations to small local weekly savings and burial clubs (see Gosden 1973).

In one sense these organised forms of working class self-help were a response to immediate conditions: to the insecurity of employment and wages, and in particular a response to a society and a state which offered only the workhouse or an inadequate amount of outdoor relief, followed by the stigma and indignity of a pauper's funeral. But as an alternative form of welfare provision, they formed a central and integrating part of working class culture. Despite their limitations and defects – their greater orientation towards male skilled workers, for example – they nevertheless embodied values of solidarity and mutual aid which were to stand in sharp contrast to the individualised self-help of bourgeois ideology. They were, moreover, organisations that were established and run by and for the workers themselves; as George Holyoake, a leading figure in the self-help movement, saw it, their essence was that through them the workers 'took their affairs into their own hands, and what is more to the point...kept them in their own hands' (cited Bonner 1961:41).

Working class self-help was not of course without ruling class support, but this should not lead us, as it has many historians (e.g. Fraser 1973; Gilbert 1964), to mistake it for a simple acceptance and reflection of bourgeois ideology. On the contrary, self-help was both an expression and a foundation of working class culture and organisation that stressed the solidarity and cohesiveness of a class (see Supple 1974; Young 1967). The very existence of such institutions, far from reflecting the ideologies of individualism and self-advancement, served as a bulwark against attempts to portray poverty as an individual failing. As one contemporary observed:

The workers still retain some ethos, especially so in homogeneous groups. They ask for a 'living wage'; they would not
'best' their fellows. This communistic consciousness of
solidarity... has resisted the teaching of Political Economy
and the Church, the (working class) proletariat is still a social
solidarity guided by moral considerations.

(Kirkman-Gray 1908:324)

There were of course exceptions: leaders and members of
Friendly Societies and trades unions who accepted the views of
middle class reformers, who epitomised individual advancement
and who argued for conciliation between labour and capital. But
we should beware of taking such views as representative of the
whole; as Charles Hardwick, one of the most 'respectable' leaders
of the largest Friendly Society himself admitted, despite his own
enthusiasm for the activities of the central government's Registrar
of Friendly Societies:

many of the members look upon him in the light of solicitor to
the government, and consequently regard with suspicion
rather than confidence any recommendations, however
valuable in themselves, which emanate from such a source.

(Hardwick 1869:147)

By the end of the nineteenth century, despite the offer of state-
guaranteed and subsidised investment as well as legal status and
protection of their funds available to any Friendly Society
registered with the state, over two-thirds remained unregistered.

Suspicion of and hostility towards the state was, like the
growth of self-help itself, a reflection of working class experience.
This experience – the experience of wage labour, of factories, and
of the state in the form of the Poor Law and the workhouse – fostered a solidarity within the working class and a
consciousness of not being part of, but rather opposed to the rest
of 'society': a consciousness which was harboured within working
class institutions and culture. Self-help was not however
revolutionary: Friendly Societies and savings banks could no
more abolish poverty than the Co-operative movement could
simply 'by-pass' capitalism. The failure of self-help directly to
confront the institution of wage labour and the inequalities of
capitalism, or to embrace the whole of the working class rather
than the more skilled and highly paid male workers, made them

essentially defensive institutions. But it was a defensiveness that stressed working class interests as separate from, rather than part of, or subordinate to the rest of society: it created 'an implicit *rival* frame, an alternative model of social relations, and a separate culture' (Young 1967:4). Far from having been success-fully incorporated within the social and political structures of society, over the turn of the century the very separateness of this culture, and its implicit suspicion of and hostility towards the state was, as we shall see, to provoke profound anxieties amongst social reformers and others for the future of social and political stability.

With the onset of mass unemployment during, the 'Great Depression' of 1873–96, the earlier hopes of increasing prosperity and political stability that had accompanied the boom of the 1840s received a severe check. 'This optimism', wrote William Beveridge in 1909, 'is broken' (Beveridge 1909:2). In its place capitalism was faced with an increasingly disillusioned and hostile working class: a working class, moreover, that had not already been incorporated into the structures and values of capitalism, but which retained its own consciousness and identity. It was this in particular that was to make the problem of unemployment and its solution a major concern, since, as George Holyoake warned, 'no protest that capital is his friend reassures him. Terror has made him deaf and experience unbelieving' (Holyoake 1878:494).

The creation of unemployment

The Great Depression of 1873–96 followed as inexorably from the boom of the 1840s as the slump of the 1920s and 1930s had followed the boom in production of the First World War or as the slump of the late 1970s and 1980s was to follow the long boom of the Second World War and its aftermath.

It is but one of the many peculiarities of capitalism that it is unable to maintain a gradual and steady trajectory of growth. Rather it has developed through alternating periods of boom and slump, a constant cycle of expansion and contraction, with approximately every fifty years a major international reversal and depression that has threatened the very basis of its economic and political stability.

The causes of this 'trade cycle' and of the major world depressions of economic activity are endemic within the system of capitalist production itself (see, for example, Sweezy 1946; Mandel 1968). Economic growth, as we have already seen, depends upon the productivity of labour, and that in turn depends upon the amount of capital–the 'means of production'–on which labour is set to work. The greater the means of production, the less labour is required to produce a given amount of goods. As some indication of this, by the mid-1980s, only one-third of the workforce was employed in what may be termed 'productive' industries, with only one-quarter employed in manufacturing, yet (and despite a general depression) producing a far greater volume of goods than a much greater proportion of the labour force had produced a hundred or even twenty years earlier.

This growing productivity of labour is one of the greatest achievements of capitalism, yet its potential to liberate human society from the struggle for existence remains denied. The growth in the means of production comes not as a relief to those in work, but as a force to dominate them and as a threat to throw them out of work. In order to compete and accumulate wealth, those who own and control capital have to produce more cheaply than their rivals; they have constantly to raise the productivity of the labour they employ, and unless they are to do this by cracking the whip harder and speeding up the machine (a solution which is frequently attempted, especially at times of economic crisis, but a solution which has very real and practical limits) they have to do it by increasing the proportion of their capital that is invested in new means of production. As Labour's Minister for Employment Albert Booth recognised in 1976, 'Expansion must depend on manufacturing industry being competitive internationally, and there is no option but to go to capital-intensive methods of production'. Yet, as he went on to recognise, 'New investment would not solve unemployment problems overnight... Some capital-intensive investment projects were yielding as little as two or three jobs for every £1 million spent' (The *Sunday Times*, September 1976).

The substitution of capital for labour, the replacement of workers by machines, has been a feature of capitalism since its origins. The decision whether to introduce 'labour-saving' machinery depends on a number of possible factors: on how 'cheap' labour is relative to the cost of machinery, or, for example, how organised and militant workers are in any particular factory or industry. Yet while in this sense the growth of capital displaces labour – while it constantly creates and recreates unemployment – this alone does not account for the sudden and periodic crises that hit all capitalist economies and throw their workers out of work. Indeed, although capital may replace labour, as it constantly did during the 1950s and 1960s, so long as capital is accumulating at a sufficiently rapid rate, it can absorb, although maybe in different occupations, industries or regions, the same and even greater amounts of labour than it employed previously.

The periodic and sudden crises in employment – the crises that see both labour and capital standing idle – are the product of a conflict between capitalism's ability to produce and what its distribution of resources allows people to consume. In order to increase productivity, as we have seen, proportionately more and more capital is invested in greater means of production, and, correspondingly, relatively less is available for the employment of labour. The two may increase together, but the former always at a more rapid rate than the latter. But since it is through wages that the effective demand for goods must come and since the total sum of wages is not rising as quickly as the rise in productivity and output, the result is that production reaches the point at which all the goods produced cannot be sold. This periodic creation of overproduction thus leads to economic stagnation and unemployment.

It is this that creates the irony of poverty amidst plenty: that sees half the world short of food, while in the other half it is stockpiled, fed to animals or simply destroyed. It has in the 1980s seen 40 million workers left without work in the industrialised countries, while industrial plant and machinery either stands idle or runs at well below its full capacity. Mass unemployment and stagnation of this nature is unique to capitalism as a system of production. In precapitalist societies, economic depression was the result of a failure of production – the result of a bad harvest, plague or natural disaster. Within capitalism, it is the result of too great a success of production: of a success that meets the limits imposed by the inequalities in the distribution of income and wealth.

The Great Depression of 1873–96 was one major example of this process of capitalist development. The expansion of industry, the opening of new markets, and the beginnings of industrial production in the United States, Europe and Japan was to cause a great flood of commodities onto the market. As competition intensified, prices began to fall, firstly in agriculture and subsequently in manufactured goods, and as the boom began to give way to stagnation, so unemployment began to rise. As Winston Churchill – as yet still in his youth – admitted, this rise could not be explained, as many attempted to do, by over-population:

> On the contrary, our wealth is increasing faster than our numbers... Enterprise in this country requires no artificial stimulus; if it errs at all, it is from time to time upon the side of overtrading and overproduction.
>
> (Churchill 1909:194)

While the 'long waves' of capitalist development have created major and catastrophic slumps in economic activity, on a world scale, with unfailing regularity over a fifty-year cycle, each slump more profound than the previous one, individual capitalist economies are also affected by their own lesser and more frequent cycle of boom and slump. Even during the overall boom following the Second World War, this 'trade cycle' was to create downturns in the economy in 1952, 1958, 1963, 1968, 1972 and, leading in to the much greater economic depression, in 1979 and 1983. Similarly, over the end of the nineteenth century, particular peaks of unemployment were to be hit in 1886, 1894, 1903 and 1908. As William Beveridge then noted:

> The outward and visible signs of an industrial depression are a high unemployed percentage and falling wages and profits. The essence of it is the inability of manufacturers to find markets at what they consider as remunerative prices.
>
> (Beveridge 1909:52)

This recognition of unemployment as, to use the title of Beveridge's pioneering book, 'A Problem of Industry' was to be a highly significant development within official understanding and thinking. It did not, as we shall see, necessarily mean that 'the personal equation', as it was called, in allocating responsibility for unemployment or in dealing with the unemployed was altogether dispensed with. Nor did it mean that the 'general ebb and flow dominating the economic life of the nation' (ibid: 41) was seen as preventable. On the contrary, official policy was to accept the inevitability of unemployment, to see in it the advantages of a disciplinary and restraining mechanism on workers and wages – 'the effect', according to Charles Booth, 'especially on wage earners is very similar to that exercised on a population by the recurrence of winter as compared to the ennervation of continual summer' (cited Stedman-Jones 1971:288) – and to seek only to deal with its more troublesome consequences.

A stirring of revolt

During the 1880s the full effect of the first Great Depression was to be felt in Britain, and as poverty and distress increased, the working class was forced to move onto the offensive. As one put it:

> Even at the best of times ... 80 per cent of the wage earners are receiving an average of 5/- per week less than is estimated as capable of supporting life decently at all ... The battle cry of the future must not be Liberalism against Toryism, but Labourism against Capitalism.
>
> (Cited Lynd 1943:292)

Or as the *Daily News* warned in 1883:

> Until lately everybody was more or less content to accept the contrast between wealth and poverty as an inexorable social law ... But we can see for ourselves at the present that every day there grows up more and more widespread the utter disbelief in the absolute necessity of existing conditions.
>
> (Cited Wohl 1968:213)

By 1886 the unemployment rate, even amongst the more securely employed trade union members for whom alone figures were available, had reached nearly ten per cent, while in certain trades such as shipbuilding and engineering it had reached over thirteen per cent. In London the situation was particularly severe. At one of the many meetings of the unemployed held in Trafalgar Square to demand work or relief the crowd broke into riot, and marched into the West End, stoning the fashionable clubs of St James and looting shops en route. The response to the Trafalgar Square riots was one of panic: for a number of days the rich lived in fear of insurrection, and shops and houses were barricaded against rumours of fresh 'invasions' of workers from the East End. The Mansion House Fund, previously a fairly moribund charity for the relief of poverty, increased its public subscription from £3,000 to £60,000 within a fortnight – a small example of what Joseph Chamberlain had the year previously described as 'the ransom which property will pay for the security which it now enjoys' (cited Saville 1957:14) – and dispensed it amongst the poor just as quickly in what Beveridge was later to call 'that orgy of relief' (Beveridge 1909:158).

The Trafalgar Square riots subsided, only to be followed by further if less dramatic demonstrations in subsequent winters in most major cities, but the riots signified the precarious stability of British society, and for many the realisation of what the Bishop of Manchester had prophesied six years earlier as:

> the strife of interests, the war of classes widening and deepening day by day ... The dull desperate hate with which those who want and have not come at last to regard the whole framework of society as but one huge contrivance for their oppression.
>
> (Cited McGregor 1957:154)

Of course 'those who want and have not' could see the wealth around them: in the ships they unloaded, the factories and warehouses where they worked, or in the homes of the bourgeoisie and middle classes where many working class women were employed as servants in the capital of what was still for a time the richest nation on earth. In many ways the East and West Ends of London symbolised this contrast between wealth and poverty – although it was a contrast that was often equally marked in many other towns and cities – but with the greatest single concentration of working people and their immediacy to the seat of national government, the problems of poverty and unemployment in London were for a time to dominate national policy.

This separation between the classes, between Disraeli's 'Two Nations', was not simply geographical, but social, cultural and ideological. As Walter Besant described it in his book *East London* in 1901:

> The population is greater than that of Berlin or Vienna, or St Petersburg or Philadelphia... In the streets there are never to be seen any private carriages; there is no fashionable quarter... one meets no ladies in the principal thoroughfares. People, shops, houses, conveyances – all together are stamped with the unmistakable seal of the working class.
>
> (Cited Stedman Jones 1971:14)

It was a world about which, at least until the 1880s, few of the rich knew or cared much at all. Yet with the rise of poverty and unemployment and its accompanying disorder and protest, there came a flood of surveys and investigations, of books, pamphlets, articles and statistics, and indeed the rise of a new 'science' of sociology, in an attempt to understand and measure the dimensions of 'the social problem' (see Abrams 1968).

Social investigation

Most of these surveys found, much to their relief, that the working class was not an homogeneous mass, but was differentiated according to levels of skill, organisation, security and wages. At the top, according to Charles Booth's mammoth survey of *The Life and Labour of the People in London*, begun in 1886, were to be found what he termed 'Class F': foremen and the self-employed, 'the higher class of labour, and the best paid of the artisans... these men are the non-commissioned officers of the industrial army' (Booth 1904:53). Beneath these was Class E: the regularly-employed workers – 'the recognised field of all forms of co-operation and combination' (ibid:51) – and when both classes were taken together, theirs 'is the standard of life on which we hope to improve, and from which, upwards or downwards, we may measure the degrees of poverty or wealth of the rest of the community' (ibid:161).

At the other end of the continuum – Booth's Classes A and B – were the chronic unemployed and the under-employed: those who had no regular employment but who depended on whatever casual work was available in the docks or in factories, supplemented by poor relief or passing charity. According to one group of social reformers – a group generally seen as being on the 'progressive' wing of the British ruling class and who were later to have a decisive influence on the formation and development of the Labour Party – these were:

> the great industrial residuum of all the industrial classes of the community, the men who have failed in life, or who, through feebleness of physique, or through want of perseverance or some hereditary incapacity, have not even succeeded in failing; the few who have lost their chance and the many who have never had a chance to lose.
>
> From this great mass of the permanently unemployed the criminal classes are recruited; from thence also the Dock Companies draw, day by day, as they require it, their casual labour... By these and other miscellaneous occupations – eked out by Mansion House Funds and other spasmodic tributes of conscience money by the rich – the unemployed of our large towns contrive to live a hand to mouth existence.
>
> (Fabian Society 1886:4)

This 'social wreckage', as Helen Bosanquet (one of the key figures in the other major social reform group of the period, the Charity Organisation Society) described them, were seen as having their own distinct – and to most social reformers unintelligible – way of life:

> What then are the characteristics of the class? Measured by the economic standard they are negative rather than positive. The ideal economic man, as we know, is remarkable for his foresight and control; in the Residuum these qualities are entirely absent. In the place of foresight we find the happy faith that 'something will turn up', and instead of self-control...impulsive recklessness... The true type of this class lives in the present moment only... His life is one incoherent jumble from beginning to end... All is aimless and drifting.
>
> (Bosanquet 1893:601)

Or, as Thomas Mackay, one of the leading advocates of a stricter Poor Law, saw it:

> It is not a question of those who fall, but rather of those who never rise, who, though they have periods of prosperity, good

and constant employment, use their advantage for making their hand-to-mouth life for the moment more profuse, and who have no conception of any other sort of life. They decline altogether to submit themselves to the teaching of the economic order. The economically disciplined classes fear poverty, and, taking some pains to avoid it, as a rule succeed in avoiding its severest forms. The main difficulty of the situation arises from the fact that for the undisciplined poverty has no terrors.

(Mackay 1902:285)

This 'resolutely proletarian attitude' (ibid) was to be held by many reformers to be the cause of the poverty of the very poor. In much the same way that sociological writings on the 'culture of poverty' in the 1960s or the intervention of politicians such as Keith Joseph, the Conservative Secretary of State for Social Services in the early 1970s, were either implicitly or explicitly to account for the persistence of poverty as the result of the attitudes or morality of the poor, so social reformers at the end of the nineteenth century were to take the means by which people live in and cope with poverty as the cause of poverty itself.

While according to Booth 'a disgrace but not a danger', the kernel of this Residuum was seen as 'perhaps incapable of improvement' (Booth 1904: 38). Together with those who 'from shiftlessness, helplessness, idleness or drink are inevitably poor' they were seen as constituting a superfluous residue – 'a deposit of those who from mental, moral and physical reasons are incapable of better work' (ibid:44). Yet what was to excite the greatest alarm and concern over the turn of the century was the revelation that destitution was not confined to this Residuum. That above them there hovered a great mass of workers – Booth's Classes C and D – 'too poor or too irregularly employed to co-operate or combine', and on whom 'falls with particular severity the weight of recurrent depressions of trade' (ibid:162). Moreover, as social reformers were increasingly to argue, the problem was not only that recurrent economic crisis threatened to depress the poor into the ranks of the very poor, but also that in doing so it risked contaminating them with the 'undisciplined' values, attitudes and behaviour of the residuum.

There had of course been earlier surveys of working class life and conditions during the nineteenth century that had revealed as much, if not more poverty, unemployment and distress as this mass of later studies was to document. But the latter fell on much more receptive ground. Whereas previous revelations may have excited curiosity, or indifference, but little concern or action, the findings of Booth and others that one-third of the working class was living below the level of subsistence now excited fear: fear for the security of property and for political stability, and fear for the future economic and military efficiency of Britain at a time when industry was stagnating and when Britain's previously undisputed role as the world's leading industrial and military power was coming under increasing challenge.

The problem of imperialism

The decline of British industry towards the end of the nineteenth century was a relative decline: a decline in the face of the emergence of the United States, Germany and soon Japan as leading industrial powers. Industrialisation, however, requires capital, and Britain, as the world's first industrial capitalist nation, was to provide much of the capital for this overseas expansion:

> As her industry sagged, her finance triumphed, her services as shipper, trader and intermediary in the world's system of payments became more indispensable. Indeed if London ever was the real economic hub of the world, the pound sterling its foundation, it was between 1870 and 1913.
>
> (Hobsbawm 1974:151)

In Britain the separation between finance and industrial capital – between the City of London and manufacturing industry – was much greater than amongst its new competitors (see Lenin 1965), and this separation as we shall see was, and has continued, to have important consequences for both domestic and foreign policy. As the Great Depression began to lift in the 1890s, although the cycle of boom and slump was to continue, British manufacturing industry found itself excluded by tariff barriers from many previous markets in the industrialising world. The City of London, however, continued to flourish: in 1873 British financiers had £1,000 million invested abroad, by 1913 £4,000 million: a total which compared with less than

£5,500 million in overseas investment held by Germany, France, Holland, Belgium and the United States put together.

Like manufacturing industry, however, British finance was also to find itself squeezed from traditional markets, and as foreign competition intensified British finance capital was to focus its attention increasingly on Britain's empire, and especially on the White Dominions of Canada, Australasia and South Africa. Faced too with the recognised ambitions in particular of German capitalism for expansion, imperialism – the cornering and securing of world markets – became an increasing necessity. As Lord Rosebery, a son-in-law of the financier Lord Rothschild and a leading figure in the Liberal Party at the time of the Boer War saw it:

> It is said that our Empire is large enough and does not need expansion. That would be true if the world were elastic, but unfortunately it is not elastic, and we are engaged at the present moment, in the language of mining, in 'pegging out our claims for the future'.

> (Cited Semmel 1960:54)

Over the turn of the century imperialism came to be seen not only as necessary for the continued growth of British capitalism, but also as a solution to the internal problems of stagnation and unemployment. As one of Britain's leading imperialists, Cecil Rhodes, explained:

> I was in the East End of London yesterday and attended a meeting of the unemployed. I listened to the wild speeches, which were just a cry for 'bread', 'bread!', and on my way home I pondered over the scene and I became more than ever convinced of the importance of imperialism.... My cherished idea is a solution for the social problem, i.e., in order to save the 40 million inhabitants of the United Kingdom from a bloody civil war, we colonial statesmen must acquire new lands to settle the surplus population, to provide new markets for the goods produced.... The Empire, as I have always said, is a bread and butter question. If you want to avoid civil war, you must become imperialists.

> (Cited Lenin 1965:93)

As a solution to the social problem, however, imperialism

required an efficient and effective army. The disastrous campaign of the Boer War, fought over the turn of the century to secure the interests of British capitalism in gold-rich South Africa, brought home to the ruling class the enormity of the problem. Not only did the incompetence of the British army and its leadership in its drawn-out attempt to defeat what was seen as little more than a handful of farmers stand in sharp contrast to the swift and decisive defeat of Tsarist Russia by the emerging industrial nation of Japan, but the recruitment campaign for the war had resulted in over half of all working class recruits having to be turned down as physically unfit to fight. The impact of prolonged unemployment and poverty was finally to be recognised as a cause for concern. As Sidney Webb, one of the leaders of the Fabian Society, put it:

> How can we build up an effective commonwealth – how even can we get an effective army – out of the stunted, anaemic, demoralised denizens of the slum tenements of our great cities?
>
> (Webb 1906:9)

What was more, the problem of imperialism was also to raise major questions for the future efficiency of British capitalism itself, for the working class provided not only an army of soldiers but also an army of labour. The physical deterioration of the working class as a result of poverty and unemployment was to force a realisation that the need to do something about it was not socialism, or even humanitarianism, but simply good business. As Prime Minister Balfour put it plainly, if bluntly, to the House of Commons:

> It is a most intolerable thing that we should permit the permanent deterioration of those who are fit for really good work. Putting aside all consideration of morals ... and looking at it with the hardest heart and the most calculating eye, is it not very poor economy to scrap good machinery?
>
> (Cited Jackson 1910:1)

The reserve armies of labour

'Unemployment is not a mere accidental blemish in a private enterprise economy' argued *The Times* in 1943, warning of the dangers of a 'full employment' economy, 'on the contrary it is part of the essential mechanism of the system and has a definite function to fulfil. The first function of unemployment, which has always existed in open or disguised forms, is that it maintains the authority of master over man' (cited Beveridge 1944:195).

Unemployment has been a constant feature of capitalism since its origins. Even during periods of a high demand for labour there has always been a number of unemployed, and in periods of exceptional demand, when the normal reserves of unemployed have come close to being used up, special efforts have had to be made to tap other more distant reserves of labour. It was this need which saw the encouragement of a migration of Irish labour in the 1840s, or of immigration from the New Commonwealth and the West Indies and the employment of married women in the 1950s and 1960s. For apart from its disciplinary func-tion – the existence of unemployment as a threat to contain the activities and wage demands of those in work – unemployment also serves a vital role in meeting the fluctuations in the demand for labour that are a characteristic of capitalist production. As Marx argued:

If a surplus labouring population is a necessary product of accumulation or the development of wealth on a capitalist basis this surplus population becomes, conversely, the lever of capitalist accumulation.... It forms a disposable reserve army that ... creates for the changing needs of the self-expansion of capital a mass of human material always ready for exploita-tion... The mass of social wealth, overflowing with the advance of accumulation... thrusts itself frantically into old branches of production or into newly formed branches... In all such cases there must be the possibility of throwing great masses of men suddenly on the decisive spots without injury to the scale of production in other spheres.

(Marx 1974:592)

The unemployed thus act as a reserve army of labour, ready to be drawn into work as production expands, and dismissed from work as it contracts. The ready availability for work of this reserve army of labour depends, however, to some extent on the particular form that it takes: forms that have to some extent varied historically and, more importantly, are distinguished according to the attitudes and ideologies surrounding them and the means by which they are maintained and provided for when not required in employment.

In its most straightforward form, the reserve army of labour is to be found in the 'floating' unemployed who move from one job to another, and for whom unemployment, even during periods of high unemployment, is usually a short-term experience. Even during periods of high unemployment such as the mid-1980s, this flow onto and off the unemployment register, although considerably slowed, still meant that one-third of the unemployed found work within a period of twelve weeks. These are the 'front line' of the reserve army of labour, usually maintained by the state at the cost of social security benefits, and under constant pressure to take whatever work is available.

The second form, which Marx called the 'latent' reserve army exists, as its name suggests, as a more hidden form of reserve. Its members are not normally counted as amongst those officially regarded as unemployed, and responsibility for their maintenance when not in employment is normally shunned by the state and where possible placed elsewhere. For such and other reasons this latent reserve is not as easily accessible to capital, although it is used whenever demand for labour is sufficient to require it. During the nineteenth century one of the major examples of such a latent reserve was to be found in the rural economy where, facing underemployment and poverty, agricultural labourers were to provide a steady stream of labour for the expansion of industry. During the course of the twentieth century, and in particular during the two world wars as well as during the post-war boom of the 1950s and 1960s, this role was to be taken on by groups such as married women and black migrant and immigrant workers. Both shared many common characteristics: in general, the cost of their production as workers and their maintenance when not in employment were borne not by the capitalist economy, but outside it, whether in the domestic economy of the family, or in the migrant worker's country of origin. Whether by law or by practice they were frequently discriminated against or excluded from the benefits of the social security system, which most particularly in the case of married women sought to place the burden of their maintenance when not in employment on their families and husbands. Surrounded by an ideology that proclaimed them as something less than 'real' workers, and facing both sexism and racism, both groups were to find themselves open to even greater exploitation in terms of working conditions and lower wages than their white, male counterparts.

The third form – described somewhat unflatteringly by Marx as the 'stagnant' reserve army – provides the final source of labour for capital's sometimes frantic bouts of expansion. The elderly, the disabled, and those previously regarded as unemployable, have all at various times been considered as fit for recruitment. Indeed, as Chris Phillipson (1982) has demonstrated, for the elderly, the concept of retirement has been a very flexible one, encouraged in a period of high unemployment, including the early 1900s when old age pensions were first introduced, and discouraged when labour has been in demand.

In such ways the various reserve armies of labour have provided an important buffer for capital. The tendency for the unemployed to be politically marginalised – whether as social security scroungers, black people, women, the elderly or disabled – serves both to legitimise and mask their greater susceptibility to unemployment and to confine them to the worst and lowest-paid jobs when they are employed. This use of the unemployed as a reserve army of labour, however, has not been without its problems. The maintenance of ideologies which legitimise discrimination against them can itself generate social and political conflict, and problems have also been created when the systems for maintaining them as a reserve army have come under strain.

The problem of casual labour

Towards the end of the nineteenth century, just as it has made a major reappearance during the closing decades of the twentieth century, one of the most widespread examples of such a reserve army was to be found in the system of casual labour. As Winston Churchill recognised:

> There is a tendency in many trades, almost in most trades, to have a fringe of casual labour on hand, available as a surplus whenever there is a boom, flung back into the pool whenever there is a slump.   (Churchill 1909:201)

Casual labour provided the means by which individual employers could maintain their own reserves of labour on hand, and through which, in the constant competition for work, wage levels could be kept to a minimum and a sharp discipline imposed on those who were taken on. As Churchill explained:

> Employers and foremen in many trades are drawn consciously or unconsciously to distribute their work among a larger number of men than they regularly require, because this obviously increases their bargaining power with them.
>
> (ibid:201)

Or as a Fabian Society report pointed out:

> It would, no doubt, be a matter of some difficulty for the Dock Companies to organise a permanent staff of labourers; such an organisation might even involve additional expenditure . . . We are, moreover, informed, upon creditable authority, that the Companies are mainly withheld from taking such a departure by the fear that the men, if once organised, might use their organisation as a lever to extract wages under the threat of strikes.
>
> (Fabian Society 1886:6)

A system of casual labour was not appropriate for all occupations, although it is estimated that up to one-third of all workers were employed on a casual basis. In the main, it was used in those sectors of the economy which required little capital investment. As Gareth Stedman Jones has argued:

> The industries which employed casual labour tended to be those most subject to arbitrary and unpredictable fluctuations in demand. Even in these industries, if labour was scarce or fixed capital formed an important proportion of the cost of production, employers had little or no incentive to casualise the labour force . . . When, however, the supply of labour was plentiful or the proportion of fixed capital was insignificant, it paid employers to adjust the size of the labour force to the exact state of demand; this might be done weekly, daily or even hourly, depending on the nature of the industry.
>
> (Stedman Jones 1971:54)

Of the employers of casual labour, the dock companies were

one of the most often-quoted examples. Dependent in the main on unskilled manual labour in an activity that fluctuated according to the tides, the weather, and the seasonal imports of commodities, each dock company encouraged its own casual labour force, from amongst which it would daily take on the number of workers it required. According to Beveridge:

> Up to the time of the great dock strike of 1889 the bulk of the work at the docks on the north of the river was performed purely by casual labourers taken on by the dock companies' foremen from a struggling crowd at the entry to each department. It was estimated that for work sufficient, if evenly distributed throughout the year, to give 3s a day to 3,000 men, at least 10,000 competed regularly.
>
> (Beveridge 1909:87)

While there was sufficient work, the system of casual labour was able to operate as a means of maintaining a reserve army, distributing work and wages in such a way as to maintain those who were casually employed at a low level of subsistence, yet organising and achieving a higher level of wages. But as the effects of economic slump were felt, both in a declining availability of work and an increased competition for it, so the system of casual labour came under increasing strain, threatening not only widespread poverty and distress, but increasing opposition and discontent.

The problem of efficiency

As the problem of unemployment began to unfold over the closing decades of the nineteenth century, so increasing attention was to be paid by social reformers, civil servants and politicians to analysing its dimensions. Yet for most, the problem was not how to abolish unemployment altogether, but how to maintain the reserve armies of labour without creating the widespread poverty and malnutrition that threatened the future viability of Britain's military and economic performance.

Here, however, a solution was not to be sought for all unemployed or underemployed workers. As one writer put it:

> The problem of unemployment is not merely the successful

curative treatment of the few thousand men who parade their degradation in street processions...Many of these men are unemployable, most are below the average ability, and their reclamation is relatively unimportant compared with the problem of providing for the vast numbers of efficient men who are deprived of work by the seasonal fluctuations of individual industries, or by the cyclical variations in the world's volume of trade.

(Jackson 1910:2)

In terms of preserving efficiency, the focus of social reformers was thus not to be on the mass of unskilled and casual workers or the chronic unemployed. Rather, concern was to focus on the skilled and regularly employed who, as a consequence of industrial depression, were falling into the ranks of the unemployed, and forced to compete for casual work, poor relief or passing charity:

Referring to our previous simile of the wheel of industry, we may say those who drop off it do not at once come under the Poor Law; their subsidence into pauperism takes a year or more. During this time, while the resources of casual jobs, pawn shops, savings and charity are exhausted in an unavailing struggle, physical or moral deterioration sets in, and the once efficient workman comes to the Poor Law, perhaps permanently enfeebled by privation and disease, perhaps a victim to drunkenness for which he is only half responsible, perhaps incurably habituated to a casual and loafing existence.

(Beveridge 1904a:28)

It was this decline into poverty and destitution of the previously skilled, efficient and regularly employed workers which was to define the economic problem of unemployment. According to Beveridge it was 'the problem of maintaining the efficiency of workers through periods of depression, the problem, in fact, of preserving the unemployed as merely "unemployed" not "unemployable"' (Beveridge 1904b:46).

In an age of imperialism concern to preserve and enhance economic and military efficiency was to be used as a powerful argument for social reform. But this greater concern for the effects of unemployment on the skilled male working class, belieing as it does the interpretation of social reform as the product of a general humanitarianism, was not simply or perhaps even mainly a reflection of the demand for greater economic efficiency. As another contemporary writer recognised:

> Not that it can be said that there is anything novel or unusual in the fact that many working men and women are laid idle through want of work. This has at all times been a regular occurrence, and it is only now, when socialist unrest by which we are surrounded has become accentuated, that attempts are being made to find 'cures' whereby the cloud of unemployment which lowers darkly over many a workman's home can be dispelled.
>
> (Hutchinson 1908:331)

Unemployment and the working class

Wage labour itself is perhaps the most important means through which a working class is disciplined and controlled. The very necessity of having to go out to work for a living, of having one's self or one's family dependent on a job, together with its often routine and deadening effect, all serve to create a powerful mechanism of social control.

Unemployment sharpens this discipline, but, and especially when it affects large numbers of workers, it also poses a potential threat to social stability. In a society where wage labour remains a major preoccupation of life, loss of employment means that the discipline of wage labour is lost. When there is little prospect of finding work, it can also become a breeding ground for disillusionment and discontent. There is of course no automatic link between unemployment and political protest. The poverty that follows unemployment may serve to dispel the illusion that capitalism is a system capable of ensuring adequate and rising living standards for all, but equally poverty can stifle protest. Organisation requires time and energy, and for a great many, especially for those for whom poverty is a chronic experience, the struggle simply to survive can consume all the energy that is available.

For such reasons periodic riots and outbursts by the poor during the nineteenth century had been seen more as a nuisance than a challenge, and dealt with more as a problem of disorder than organised resistance. As *The Guardian* argued in 1885, organised socialism 'had never been able to touch the miserable poor, and had always been most successful in converting the well-to-do and intelligent artisans' (cited Pelling 1968:58). But as the effects of economic depression spread to affect the more skilled and organised workers, so there emerged, as Gareth Stedman Jones has argued, 'the dangerous possibility ... that the respectable working class, under the threat of prolonged unemployment, might throw in its lot with the casual poor' (Stedman Jones 1971:284).

The formation in 1882 of the revolutionary Social Democratic Federation, which was to concentrate much of its work on organising the unemployed, and the Trafalgar Square riots of 1886 both revealed this danger. As one contemporary observed recalled the events of 1886:

> On Friday the 7th of October last, it somehow occurred to the minds of six or seven half-crazy loons, bitten by the tarantula of social democracy, to go at midnight to Trafalgar Square and preach the new gospel of discontent to the starvelings there ... Next day they unfurled the red flag of revolution in the square, and meetings and processions were openly begun. At first the majority of their listeners were shiftless flotsam and jetsam of the community. Day by day ... the numbers increased of the more respectable workmen ... The mob had now become articulate and capable of suggesting ways of extending the existing system of relief.
>
> (Burleigh 1887:773)

That the organised working class was capable of giving leadership to the unorganised was only one of the political aspects of the problem of unemployment. The closing decades of the nineteenth century were to see a growing political consciousness and new forms of organisation amongst the working class. Amongst these was the rise of new forms of trades unionism, in particular amongst unskilled workers. This new unionism, epitomised in the match girls' strike or the formation of the dockworkers' union was very different from the older exclusively male and craft-based forms of trades union organisation. It organised workers across different occupations and industries, appealing to workers in terms of their class rather than their occupation. In the place of the defensiveness and exclusivity of the craft unions, it saw itself in open confrontation with capital.

This growth of working class consciousness and organisation was to make the problem of unemployment a much more difficult problem for capital or the state to deal with. As John Burns, a former leader of the dock workers in their successful struggle to form a trade union and previous member of the Social Democratic Federation wrote in 1906, the unemployed had formerly been 'patient, long-suffering, mute, inarticulate ...' but now:

> the extension of the franchise, education, trade unionism, Socialist propaganda, the broad and rising labour movement have altered all this. The unemployed worker of today is of different stuff. He has a grievance, and thinks he has a remedy.
>
> (Burns 1906:4)

A belief in socialism was by no means universal amongst the working class at the end of the nineteenth century, but then neither was the dissatisfaction of socialists confined to those who considered themselves as such. The experience of unemployment and poverty had, for many, strained the belief that capitalism could, as its more ardent supporters promised, offer security and prosperity. As Haldane, a leading member of the Liberal Party was forced to admit in 1888:

> We cannot ignore the magnitude and importance of the problem with which Karl Marx and the Socialists have sought to deal in so courageous a fashion. The existing relation of capital and labour, and the consequent distribution of wealth, is in need of far-reaching improvement.
>
> (Cited Brown 1964:16)

We shall see in the next chapter what sort of improvement was to be made. In the meantime, the attention of social reformers was to focus on the working class itself, in the attempt to gauge its political temper. As they discovered, socialism, at least in its conscious and organised forms, was most widespread amongst the skilled working class. 'It is here', argued Booth in relation to his Classes E and F, 'that we find the springs of Socialism and Revolution' (Booth 1904:308), while another writer noted how:

the most advanced section desires to get rid of the state itself, as barring the free action of the individual, and aims at self-governing social organisation.

(Anon 1889:264)

As we have seen, this attitude of hostility towards the state was not confined to the socialist movement, but was a widespread and essential, if less articulated, feature of working class culture and organisation. According to the Assistant Secretary of the Ancient Order of Foresters, the second largest and generally considered one of the most 'respectable' of working class Friendly Societies, proposals for state-subsidised old age pensions were:

no doubt considered a very alluring bait to obtain the support of the Friendly Societies; but concealed under the bait, to use an angler's illustration, is an insidious hook, which would drag us out of the free waters of self-dependence and land us on the enervating bank of State control.... It may be depended upon as a solid truth that the State will not grant us special privileges without wanting to have a finger in our pie.

(Cited Chamberlain 1892:607)

By the end of the nineteenth century, the Friendly Society movement, catering for over half the working class population, was in a state of crisis. Burdened by rising unemployment and the need to pay out increasing amounts in benefit on the one hand, and by a growing inability of their members to maintain their contributions on the other, they nevertheless resisted offers of state subsidy or attempts to relieve them of the burden by the provision of state pensions. Such 'bribes' were, in the words of the Chief High Ranger of the Ancient Order of Foresters, no more than attempts to deprive the working class of:

the best right of Englishmen – the right of independence, of self-government – which should not be bartered away for a mess of pottage... Care must be taken that the rising generations are not enticed by bribes drawn from the pockets of those who esteem their freedom, or forced by legislative compulsion to exchange the stimulating atmosphere of independence and work for an enervating system of mechanical obedience to State management and control – the certain sequel to State subsidy.

(Cited Treble 1970:274)

Such opposition to the state cannot be seen simply as stemming from 'essentially mundane motives' (Treble 1970:274), or from an attachment to 'ideals of Victorian individualism' (Gilbert 1964:558). Certainly most working class self-help was not revolutionary, nor was much of it explicitly socialist. But the values of independence, self-reliance and co-operation which it defended and embodied, and its view of the state as part of the oppressive mechanism of a ruling class, provided a rich culture in which a socialist and oppositional ideology could develop. With rising unemployment and poverty amongst the working class, this culture was to prove potentially explosive. It was also to focus increasing working class criticism on the system of poor relief. As Sidney Webb argued in 1890:

> It becomes increasingly obvious that popular feeling cannot be relied upon to uphold any rigid refusal of outdoor relief, even to the able-bodied.
>
> (Webb 1890:96)

In the form of a deterrent Poor Law, the state had only one mechanism for relieving working class poverty. As more workers were forced to experience its stigma and humiliation, and in particular as it was experienced by those more skilled, organised and politically conscious workers who had previously had little or no contact with it, so the entire system and principles of poor relief were in danger of being swept away. It was this, above all else, that was to lead to proposals to provide more lenient treatment for those who were seen as the 'deserving' poor. As the Report of the Royal Commission on the Aged Poor, for example, argued:

> We are convinced by the evidence that there is a strong and prevalent feeling in favour of greater discrimination, especially in the case of the aged, between the respectable poor, and those whose poverty is distinctly the result of their own misconduct. Unless this distinction is more clearly recognised than it has hitherto been, we fear that the agitation against the whole policy of the Poor Law may gain in strength.
>
> (Cited Local Government Board *Annual Report* 1895:298)

This concern to distinguish between the 'respectable' and the chronic poor and unemployed was to dominate the problem of poverty and unemployment and the search for its solution. It was a response to a blurring of the divisions and distinctions within the working class, and was to see attempts by social investigators and reformers to reinstate such divisions. As Charles Booth put it:

> The question of those who actually suffer from poverty should be considered separately from that of the true working classes, whose desire for a larger share of the wealth is of a different character. It is the plan of agitators and the way of sensational writers to confound the two in one, to talk of 'starving millions', and to tack on the thousands of the working classes to the tens or hundreds of distress. Against this method I protest. To confound these essentially distinct problems is to make the solution of both impossible. It is not by welding distress and aspirations that any good can be done.
>
> (Booth 1904:155)

It was precisely this welding of distress and aspirations which constituted the political problem of unemployment: the threat of an increasingly hostile, organised and cohesive working class which refused to accept existing conditions as natural or inevitable and which threatened, if something was not done about it, to overthrow the existing structure and social relations of society. As Winston Churchill warned:

> The greatest danger to the British people is not to be found among the enormous fleets and armies of the European continent... It is here, close at home, close at hand in the vast growing cities of England and Scotland, and in the dwindling and cramped villages of our denuded countryside. It is here you will find the seeds of imperial ruin and national decay – the unnatural gap between rich and poor, the divorce of the people from the land, the want of proper training and discipline in our youth, the awful jumbles of an obsolete Poor Law, the constant insecurity in the means of subsistence and employment... Here are the enemies of Britain. Beware lest they shatter the foundations of her power.
>
> (Churchill 1909:363)

four

SOCIAL REFORM

The Poor Law; the reform of charity; relief work; the role of experts; Fabianism and eugenics; emigration and labour colonies; the Unemployed Workman Act; liberalism and social reform; the role of the Labour Party; two forms of imperialism; socialism and social reform; social reform and the working class; administrative reform; labour exchanges and the mobile reserve army of labour; National Insurance.

> That is the doctrine of reformers. We seek to cleanse, to repair, to strengthen private property...
>
> (A. Arnold 'Socialism and the unemployed' 1888:59)

Social reform was a response to the problems of unemployment and poverty. It was a response which identified the need for a reform of social relations and conditions – a 'corresponding change of tactics'– as an attempted solution to the problems of over-production: of waste and inefficiency, of the growing discontent of the working class and the threat of socialism.

As a class, however, those who own and control the means of production and wealth do not always act in unison. They are themselves divided by competition; they offer differing views and explanations of the problems they face; and they differ in the manner and degree to which they are prepared to undertake reform. As one writer argued at the beginning of the century, there were many:

> who would resist all attempts at reform in industrial conditions, lest they be deemed concessions in the nature of a surrender, would dam higher a rising stream to prevent it becoming uncontrollable, blindly contributing to the disaster which must ensue.
>
> (Lewis 1909:39)

Fear that social reform would appear as a surrender to labour were indeed widespread amongst the ruling class, and this as we shall see was to be an important factor in the timing of social reform. As John Saville has argued:

> The question of timing was, and is crucial; for what may be a major victory for the working class at one point in time and which may well lead to significant changes in the internal balance of political forces within the country, is not necessarily of the same importance when it has been long delayed.
> (Saville 1957:11)

But while the bourgeoisie were eventually to face the necessity of reform, they had first to be persuaded not only of the type of changes required, but also that they had a common interest in pursuing them.

This task of persuasion was to be undertaken by that group of people who identified themselves as social reformers. Some, like Charles Booth the Liverpool shipping merchant, Joseph Chamberlain the Birmingham manufacturer, or Seebohm Rowntree, were themselves employers of labour or owners of property from which they secured an income. Others were to be drawn from the rapidly expanding new 'middle' class of intellectuals, professional politicians and civil servants who, according to Marx:

> stand in the middle between the workers on the one side and the capitalists and landed proprietors on the other, who are for the most part supported directly by revenue, who rest as a burden on the labouring foundation, and who increase the social security and power of the upper ten thousand.
> (Cited Nicolaus 1967:45)

In formulating proposals that were in the longer-term interest of the survival of capitalism social reformers were at times to come into conflict with sections of their own class. Social reform was no minor undertaking. It threatened many vested interests, challenged much political orthodoxy, and, like most attempts to reform and to increase the efficiency of capitalism, it was a policy which could best be afforded by and stood most to benefit the interests of large-scale over small employers. As Beatrice Webb recognised:

What we have to do is to detach the great employer, whose profits are too large to feel the immediate pressure of regulation and who stands to gain by increased efficiency, from the ruck of small employers or stupid ones. What seems clear is that we shall get no further instalments of social reform unless we gain the consent of an influential minority of the threatened interest.

(Cited Saville 1957:9)

Social reformers, however, were not an homogeneous group. While they were to share many ideas on the nature of the problem and on the purposes of social reform, they were also to differ in their views on the manner in which reform was to be undertaken and achieved. As a result, the progress of reform was to be characterised by differing levels of response and solution to 'the social problem', ranging from those who wished merely to strengthen existing methods of disciplining the working class, to those who were to argue for more subtle, more comprehensive and more far-reaching schemes.

What was eventually to distinguish the progressive wing of social reformers – who finally were to triumph in the flood of social reform introduced between 1908 and 1911 – from the more orthodox and traditional wing was to be its attitude to the state, and in particular the willingness to adopt what were seen as more radical and positive forms of state intervention in order to preserve both capitalism and the state itself in the face of the escalation of class conflict. In this task they built upon the activities of those social reformers in the early part of the nineteenth century who, through measures such as public health provision, factory regulation and inspection, the creation of a police force and Poor Law reform, laid down the structures of the modern state. What progressive and radical social reformers were now to do was to adapt these structures to meet the challenge of organised labour, and in so doing to create a set of practices and policies and an ideology – of social democracy, of citizenship, and of the neutrality of the state – that was to endure well into the twentieth century.

The Poor Law

One of the first reactions to the growing problem of poverty and unemployment was a move to strengthen the existing methods of discipline and control. Such moves have tended to characterise all periods of steeply rising unemployment and distress. The beginning of slump in the 1920s, for example, saw the intro-duction of the Genuinely Seeking Work test (Deacon 1976), while the escalation of unemployment from the late 1970s was similarly accompanied by severe restrictions on benefit and attempts to refashion the social security system in 1980 and 1986. Faced with increasing unemployment, the state has never responded simply by expanding relief, and even where conces-sions have been given, these have often been given with one hand and taken away with the other. Almost as if in anticipation of what is to come, and certainly as a means of restricting commitment and expenditure and deterring applications for relief, the state has responded to the onset of crisis by bearing down harshly on claimants in a futile attempt to stem the tide.

Such was true of the early 1870s, when rising unemployment and poverty was met with an attempt to adhere more strictly to the workhouse regime. Despite the ideal of the Poor Law Commissioners of 1834, the total abolition of outdoor relief, at least to the able-bodied unemployed, had remained an impossi-bility. Confronted with working class opposition, as well as the impracticality of the workhouse for dealing with sudden and massive fluctuations in unemployment, the Commission and its successors had had little choice but to allow the majority of able-bodied applicants to receive outdoor relief. That the granting of a small amount of outdoor relief was much cheaper than institu-tionalisation was, often to the consternation of the Poor Law Commission, also a point not lost on many Boards of Guardians. The workhouse had continued to be a place of maintenance, and deterrence, primarily for the old, the sick, unmarried mothers and children (Webb 1929:134).

When, however, the Local Government Board took over responsibility for the Poor Law in 1871, a campaign was begun to abolish outdoor relief to the able-bodied and return to the principles of 1834 (see Smart 1909). As part of this campaign a number of special 'Test Workhouses' were established specifi-cally for the able-bodied male unemployed, to which other Poor Law Unions were invited to send the unemployed as a 'test' of their destitution. The first was established in the London working class borough of Poplar in 1871; in the eight years of its operation 154 inmates were sentenced to imprisonment and 1,081 placed in solitary confinement on bread and water for refusing to submit to its regime (Report 1909 III:473). The experiment was considered by the authorities to be a 'success'; despite mounting unemployment and distress, fear of receiving an 'Order for Poplar' deterred thousands from applying for help. As the Local Government Board noted with pride in its second Annual Report:

> The result appears to have been satisfactory... Notwithstanding the considerable number of Unions which have availed themselves of this privilege, the number...who have accepted relief, or having accepted it have remained in the workhouse, has been so small that, although the workhouse will contain 788 persons, there were in it, at the close of last year, only 166 inmates. Great credit appears to be due to the Guardians of the Poplar Union for the firm and judicious manner in which they have conducted this, the first experiment of its kind.
>
> (Cited Webb 1929:380)

Further experiments of this kind were introduced in Birmingham in 1880, in Kensington in 1882, and in Manchester and Sheffield. Their eventual abandonment was the result of a mixture of public hostility and opposition (in Poplar even the police refused to sanction prosecutions demanded by the workhouse master), the expense of maintaining a practically empty workhouse, and the growing practice by which other Unions used the opportunity to unload onto the Test Workhouse not only their able-bodied unemployed, but also the sick, the elderly and the infirm.

What other, and supposedly more 'enlightened' reformers also recognised was that such crudely deterrent measures simply shifted the problem elsewhere:

> What an able-bodied Test Workhouse does is to keep these wastrels and cadgers off the rates – at the cost of leaving them to roam about at large and indulge in their expensive and demoralising parasitism, a danger to property and the public, and a perpetual trouble to the police... The able-bodied... were presumably to be face to face with the alternatives of

either working or starving. As a matter of fact our social organisation is still too loose to narrow their choice to any such extent.

(Webb 1929:394)

Such consequences have of course continued to be the effect of a policy that deals with rising levels of distress and claims for state support simply by pushing people off benefit. As David Donnison, head of the Supplementary Benefits Commission until 1980 admitted, although considerable numbers of claimants fall foul of the cohabitation rule or of various 'tests' of the unemployed, and are refused or cease to claim benefit, 'what happens to them afterwards is something we know much less about'. Yet the rise in particular of property crime that has followed increasing poverty and unemployment in the 1980s is more than just coincidence. While a policy of deterrence has its first effect in increasing hardship and suffering, it also pushes the problem elsewhere: predominantly onto families, but also into crime and other ways of making out which the 'looseness' of social organisation affords. For, much though it has achieved, capitalism has never fully been able to remove all alternatives to wage labour. At the end of the nineteenth century, one of the most significant of these alternatives was the existence of charity.

The reform of charity

Charity was the most immediate and obvious response of the bourgeoisie as a class to the problems of poverty and unemployment. Whether elicited through sympathy or fear, the giving of money was an instinctive response to working class destitution and, as the blossoming of the Mansion House Fund after the Trafalgar Square riots had shown, a barometer of working class unrest. By 1870 charitable expenditure in London alone amounted to some £7 million a year, or three-and-a-half times as much as was spent in Poor Law relief.

This predominance of charitable and philanthropic activity in London has been explained in terms of the particular economic and social relations that distinguished London from most other urban areas (Stedman Jones 1971). Like a small number of other cities, most notably Liverpool (which, significantly, was also to contribute more than its share of social reformers), these relations arose out of the absence of any significant large-scale industrial content to the metropolitan economy and its domination by a ruling class whose income derived largely from finance and trade. With its mass of casual and seasonal labour in the docks and markets, together with the sharp geographical separation between the east and west ends, this lack of personal and day-to-day contact between the rich and poor posed particular problems as to how the poor were to be controlled.

In responding to this problem charity for the most part consisted merely of the handing out of money in response to periodic crises of distress and revolt. As a way of buying off working class discontent, however, charity was to come under increasing scrutiny and criticism. According to Helen Bosanquet, one of the leading figures of the Charity Organisation Society:

> Soup kitchens, philanthropic societies, country holiday funds, ragged school funds, funds from all the enterprising newspapers, and funds from all the political clubs in the district; church funds and chapel funds, missions and mothers' meetings, all are engaged in pouring money into a slough of poverty, which swallows it up and leaves no trace of improvement.
>
> (Bosanquet 1896:37)

The Charity Organisation Society, as its name suggests, was established in 1869 with the aim of organising all charitable activity, of putting it on what it saw as a footing more appropriate to an urban industrialised society, and of educating the bourgeoisie and its middle class in the dangers of indiscriminate alms-giving (see Jones 1978). As one of its members put it to them:

> If you are going to do nothing else, if you are going to satisfy your conscience on the one hand, and provide a doubtful safety-valve against social upheaval on the other, by lavish charity, then I say it would be better to let the destitute – men, women and children – die of cold and hunger on the street.
>
> (Cited Jones 1978:71)

The attitude and activity of the C.O.S. stemmed from a belief, summed up by its own monthly journal the *Charity Organisation Review* that 'the poverty of the working classes in England is due, not to their circumstances (which are more favourable than those of any other working population in Europe) but to their own improvident habits and thriftlessness. If they are ever to be more prosperous, it must be through self-denial, temperance and forethought' (ibid:50). In short, poverty was a problem of character; hence to solve poverty required a change not in material circumstances, but in the habits and character of the poor.

The problem with indiscriminate charity, as the C.O.S. saw it, was that it merely pandered to this deficiency. To provide money and relief at times of distress was to absolve the working class from the responsibility of making its own provision; it was to encourage dependency and to discourage thrift and self-reliance. It was, moreover, a danger which threatened not only those in receipt of charity but also by example to undermine the precarious independence and discipline of the working class as a whole.

The ideology that poverty was a product of character, that the destitute through a lack of discipline, hard work and thrift were responsible for their own situation, was not new. Neither was it a view held only by the C.O.S. As the Fabian Society also argued, 'Almsgiving of whatever kind – crude, spasmodic, and ill-directed as it generally is – produces all the evil effects of gambling or lotteries upon a race too little inclined by training and hereditary influences to hard work' (Fabian Society 1886:5). But it was an ideology that was to find in the C.O.S. its most coherent and consistent champion. From it the C.O.S. was to criticise its own class for their short-sighted attempts to find 'easy' solutions to the social problem, in much the same way that Margaret Thatcher was later to criticise employers for their unwillingness to take a sufficiently tough approach.

The influence of the C.O.S. was to be pervasive and significant. But its importance did not lie only in its critique of indiscriminate charity. While poverty and destitution were seen as a moral failing, as the effects of the trade depression and unemployment bit deeper, so the C.O.S. recognised that increasing numbers of those who swelled the ranks of the residuum were workers who had previously been in permanent employment, who might well have attempted to save and to avoid poor relief, but who under the weight of circumstances were now broken by adversity.

It was to this group that the C.O.S. was to direct its attention. The chronic unemployed and the habitual receivers of poor relief and charity, they regarded as superfluous, as a class which was purely parasitic, and whose absence of the virtues of thrift and self-reliance placed them beyond hope or possibility of redemption. To provide them with charity was merely to prolong their existence, and to sustain them as a source of infection and moral contagion to those who fell into their ranks. The only appropriate way of dealing with them was through a rigorous application of the Poor Law and workhouse test. Those, on the other hand, who displayed evidence of previous character, and for whom destitution was to be considered a temporary lapse, were to be the true objects of 'scientific charity' and to be helped by charitable effort to regain their independence. Organised charity was thus 'to take care of the deserving poor ... the profligate and the improvident should be left to the sterner rule of the Poor Law and the workhouse test' (Charity Organisation Review. Cited Jones op cit:14).

In accordance with its aim of organising charity according to its own principles, the C.O.S. was to establish itself as a major reform institution, with local offices in every London borough and in most other large cities, staffed by voluntary workers whose task was to control and direct charity, to investigate and sift applicants for assistance, and through personal supervision to restore the deserving poor back to independence and self-reliance.

This attempt to transform charity from its semi-feudal connotations to an effective and efficient means of social control was not to be wholly successful, and in its procedures of investigation and moral classification, the C.O.S. was to meet with profound hostility and opposition from within the working class. Eventually its attempts to solve the problems of unemployment and poverty through individual example and voluntary effort were to be overtaken by an approach that argued for the more direct intervention of the state. But as a 'school' of social reformers - through which many were to pass – its influence on social policy was to be considerable, extending through subsequent legislation to its domination of the 1909 Poor Law Commission, and

establishing a tradition, philosophy and practice that was subsequently to form the basis for the contemporary practice of social
work (see Jones 1983).

Relief work

While the C.O.S. was ultimately to fail to dominate social reform
strategies, its arguments, in particular on the need to discriminate between what it saw as deserving and undeserving cases,
were to have considerable impact. In the eyes of many social
reformers, the C.O.S. had 'taught the country the importance of
doing a work which private funds cannot despatch' (Kirkman-
Grey 1908:293), and the search was to continue for ways of
discriminating in the relief of the poor and the unemployed.
What was to make the period from the 1880s onwards a turning-
point in the history of social security was the recognition that
this discrimination could not be effected within the Poor Law
itself, or between the Poor Law and voluntary charity, but
required new forms of state relief in order 'to segregate the
unemployable and enable more to be done to keep the decent
workman from deterioration' (Jackson and Pringle 1909:135).

The riots of the unemployed in Trafalgar Square in 1886
signalled the beginnings of this change. Four weeks later the
Local Government Board under Joseph Chamberlain issued the
famous 'Chamberlain Circular' to all Boards of Guardians and
local authorities:

> The Local Government Board...are convinced that in the
> ranks of those who do not ordinarily seek Poor Law relief
> there is evidence of much and increasing privation, and if the
> depression in trade continues, it is to be feared that large
> numbers of persons usually in regular employment will be
> reduced to the greatest straits.
>
> Such a condition of things is a subject for deep regret and
> very serious consideration.
>
> The spirit of independence which leads so many of the
> working classes to make great personal sacrifices rather than
> incur the stigma of pauperism is one which deserves the
> greatest sympathy and respect, and which it is the duty and
> interest of the community to maintain by all the means at its

disposal... It is not desirable that the working classes should be familiarised with Poor Law relief, and if once the honourable sentiment which leads them to avoid it is broken down it is probable that recourse will be had to this provision on the slightest occasion.

(Cited in Appendix to Alden 1905)

Accordingly the Circular authorised the provision of temporary relief work 'which will not involve the stigma of pauperism', although, 'in order to prevent imposture and to leave the strongest temptation to those who avail themselves of this opportunity to return as soon as possible to their previous occupations, the wages paid should be something less than the wages ordinarily paid for similar work' (ibid).

These municipal relief works, outside of the auspices of the Poor Law, were to be provided for those 'skilled artisans and others... who have hitherto avoided Poor Law assistance... and whom, owing to previous condition and circumstances, it is undesirable to send to the workhouse or to treat as subjects for pauper relief.' Relief works were thus not a strategy designed to supersede the Poor Law altogether. On the contrary, they were designed to provide only for the more skilled and organised of the unemployed who were seen as threatening to identify their lot with that of the casual and chronic poor.

Such a strategy was not only concerned to forestall the growing alienation of the organised working class. Large-scale unemployment and poverty present particular problems for capitalism, not least of which is to undermine the ideology that poverty and unemployment are peripheral problems largely the fault of the poor and the unemployed themselves. If this ideology was to be upheld, and the punitive treatment and discipline of the reserve armies of casual and residual poor maintained, the separation and provision of more lenient treatment for those whose unemployment was seen as only temporary and exceptional was a matter of urgent necessity. As Chamberlain revealed confidentially in a letter to Beatrice Webb:

It will remove one great danger, viz. that public sentiment should go wholly over to the unemployed, and render impossible that state sternness to which you and I equally attach much importance... By offering reasonable work at low wages we may secure the power of being very strict with the loafer and the confirmed pauper.

(Cited Harris 1972:76)

While the establishment of relief works were to dominate responses to the problem of unemployment for the next twenty years, they were to come under increasing criticism. As the C.O.S.-dominated Majority Report of the Royal Commission on the Poor Laws was later to argue, 'it seems clear that no effective measures were taken by the municipalities, as a whole, to ensure that they should confine their relief of the unemployed to the particular class of workmen suggested' (Report 1909, Vol I:484).

Few authorities were able to deal with the issue of discrimination systematically, or to exclude the chronic unemployed and casual labourers. Dependent as they were on local rates for their finance, those working class districts with the highest unemployment and greatest need often had the least resources to carry them out. The amount of money considered necessary for supervision and training also made relief works extremely expensive – of over £11,000 spent by the London Borough of Islington in using the unemployed for street paving, less than £2,500 was paid in actual relief. Furthermore, the massive number of workers applying for relief work often meant that it was spread so thinly as to have little effect; in Bermondsey, for example, during the winter of 1904/5 the amount of work provided for each applicant averaged only three days in five months (C.O.S. 1908:58). As a result, according to the 1909 Royal Commission:

Municipal relief works have not assisted but rather prejudiced the better class of workmen they were intended to help. On the other hand they have encouraged the casual labourers by giving them a further supply of that casual work which is so dear to their hearts and so demoralising to their character.

(Report 1909, Vol I:489)

By failing to exclude the casual and long-term unemployed, and, as Beveridge put it, 'by setting a standard of output by the ability of the weakest or idlest member' (Beveridge 1909:156), relief works were to be regarded as a failure. At a time when concern over national efficiency was to reach almost hysterical proportions, they were seen as doing little to arrest the physical decline of a skilled but unemployed working class. As a form of relief, moreover, relief work was viewed not as having solved the problem of demoralisation and unrest, but as itself contributing to the devaluation of labour discipline. As the Charity Organisation Society argued:

> The work was even more demoralising than the ordinary casual employment to be obtained under industrial conditions, for it ceased to be necessary for the workman to render an equivalent in service for the wage paid.
>
> (C.O.S. 1908:36)

Such criticisms were to be equally levied against the programme of relief works established during the 1930s, and were to be a spur to the continual revision of relief work programmes under the Manpower Services Commission in the 1970s and 1980s, just as they had been made by the Poor Law Commissioners at the beginning of the nineteenth century:

> Relief and wages are confounded. The wages partake of relief, and the relief partakes of wages. The labourer is employed, not because he is a good workman, but because he is a parishioner. He receives a certain sum, not because it is the fair value of his labour, but because it is what the vestry has ordered to be paid.
>
> (Report 1834:167)

The role of experts

Over the turn of the century, the concern to discriminate between different groups of the unemployed was to be given new impetus. The revelation of widespread malnutrition amongst the working class produced by the recruitment campaign for the Boer War, striking as it did fears for Britain's international and industrial decline, was to produce a campaign within the ruling class for national efficiency (see Searle 1971). It was a campaign that was to have far-reaching implications, setting high on the political agenda the need to do something about the problems of poverty and unemployment. It was to focus attention not only on the consequences of poverty for the unemployed, and the implications this had for industry and empire, but also on the condition of working class families and the role of women as mothers of a future generation (see Davin 1978; Langan and Schwarz 1985). It was also to challenge the amateurism that has long been a characteristic of the British ruling class, and allow social reformers to argue for recognition of their own expertise in developing 'scientific' solutions to the social problem.

In this respect, although they were at different ends of the political spectrum of ruling class opinion, both the Fabian Society and the Charity Organisation Society shared common ground in their distrust not only of well-intentioned amateurs and 'do-gooders', but often also of politicians themselves. As Helen Bosanquet argued:

> Perhaps the greatest obstacle to getting a sound opinion on matters of social policy lies in the general ignoring of the fact that scientific principles are as much involved in them as chemistry or architecture, or any other of the arts of life.
>
> (Cited Jones 1976:18)

Similarly, the leading figures in the Fabian Society complained that:

> Our governing classes ... do not yet seem to have realised that social reconstruction requires as much specialised training and sustained study as the building of bridges and railways, the interpretation of the law, or the technical improvements in machinery and mechanical progress.
>
> (Webb 1911:18)

In the view of both organisations, the social reconstruction and reform of capitalism could not be left to novices. But 'science' and 'expertise', at least in this context, are not neutral terms. In the first place, the analysis of poverty and of the dangers of relief developed by both societies contained an implicit class bias. As George Lansbury, who with the extension of the franchise was to come to head a working class majority on the Board of Guardians in Poplar argued:

> I have no desire to see men and women struggle on and refuse to come to their fellows for help, for I have never yet seen any disposition on the part of the middle and upper classes to do so. Cabinet Ministers who have been in receipt of £5,000 a year

take their pension of £1,300 a year without any dread of its
pauperising effect.

(Lansbury 1903:8)

In the second place, the promotion of expertise was a political
development that was to be profoundly anti-democratic and that
was increasingly to deny to working class people both the
legitimacy and the means to define and solve the problems that
they themselves faced. With respect to Poplar, the Guardians'
refusal to adopt the workhouse test or the principle of less
eligibility was to lead to demands that poor relief should be taken
out of democratic control and put into the hands of 'experts'. As
the Majority Report of the Royal Commission on the Poor Laws
put it:

> Under the present method of direct election ... there is no
> security that the Guardians elected will be those who are most
> suited to the position. The work is tending more and more to
> fall into the hands of persons who ... direct their administra-
> tion more towards the attainment of popularity than towards
> the solution of the real problems of pauperism. We shall
> recommend that in future the members of the Local Authority
> shall be largely nominated from amongst men and women of
> experience, wisdom, and unselfish devotion to the public
> good.

(Report 1909; Vol I:145)

As we shall see later, the protection of 'the public good' from
public accountability and control – the removal of poor relief and
subsequent social security administration from democratic influence – was to have to wait until the 1930s, when the spread of
'Poplarism' was to create a major political confrontation between
the working class and the state.

Fabianism and eugenics

In the meantime both the Charity Organisation Society and the
Fabian Society were to continue to press their demands to be
recognised by the rest of the ruling class as the ultimate
authority on social reform. The difference between the two
organisations was ultimately one of means rather than ends, for
as Sidney Webb argued the aim of Fabianism, like that of the

C.O.S., was 'that creation of individual character, which is the real goal of all collective effort' (Webb 1890:97).

Whereas for the C.O.S. the remodelling of individual character could only be achieved through voluntary effort and example, for the Fabian Society this could only be achieved by the state. In its view the inevitable inequalities and inefficiencies of an unregulated capitalism could only be solved by the rational, conscious and scientific control of private industry and the re-moralisation of the working class achieved through the creation of a powerful body of state institutions, officials and experts concerned with the maintenance, education and disciplining of labour. While this radical agenda for state interference and involvement in the affairs of private capital was to lead it to be identified as 'socialist', it was what Marx had called a form of 'bourgeois socialism' that did not seek to overthrow the major institutions of capitalism, but rather sought to use the power of the state to make it more efficient. As one Fabian member described their project:

> The aims of modern socialism may be described as an endeavour to readjust the machinery of industry in such a way that it can at once depend upon and issue in a higher kind of character and social type than is encouraged by the conditions of ordinary competitive enterprise ... The absence of any permanent organisation of industry, by setting a premium on partial and discontinuous employment, is itself a contributory cause of shiftless character; and where the character is hopeless, the best way of dealing with it is such an organisation as would really sift out and eliminate the industrial residuum.
>
> (Ball 1906:18)

'Science', moreover, painted an even more alarming picture, for this was an era that saw the introduction of eugenics into social policy, the theories of biological evolution and of social Darwinism that portrayed a world in which the progress of nations was a process of selection headed by the survival of the fittest. Accompanied by an imperialist and racist policy and ideology, these theories were to be applied to Britain also, where a large and growing class of unfit labour was seen as a drain on Britain's struggle for survival in an increasingly competitive world (see Semmel 1960). These theories also were to be used to press the case for state intervention in a radical reshaping of the system of relief. As Sidney Webb argued:

> The policy of *laissez-faire* is, necessarily, to a eugenicist the worst of all policies, because it implies the definite abandonment of intelligently purposeful selection... The question of who is to survive is determined by the conditions of the struggle, the rules of the ring. Where the rules of the ring favour a low type, the low type will survive, and vice versa... It is accordingly our business, as eugenicists, deliberately to manipulate the environment so that the survivors may be of the type which we regard as the highest.
>
> (Webb 1910/11:234)

The existing Poor Law, however, in relieving the destitute, 'operates almost exclusively as an anti-eugenic device' (ibid). In a theme that was to continue to be and is currently echoed in a number of areas of social policy the very poor were branded with an ideology that saw them as diseased and contagious, requiring at best drastic social engineering, and at times elimination. Such views, moreover, were not confined to the Fabian Society; the supposed humanitarianism of social reformers often found its limits when addressing this issue. As Charles Booth saw it:

> The difficulties, which are great, do not lie in the cost. As it is, these unfortunate people cost the community one way or another considerably more than they contribute... If they were ruled out we should be better off than we are now; and if this class were under State tutelage – say at once under State slavery – the balance-sheet would be more favourable to the community.
>
> (Booth 1904:165)

For Beveridge, often regarded as the founder of the 'welfare' state, the solution was even more final:

> The line between independence and dependence, between the efficient and the unemployable, has to be made clearer and broader... [The latter] must become the acknowledged dependants of the State, removed from industry and maintained adequately in public institutions; but with complete and permanent loss of all citizen rights – including not only the franchise, but civil freedom and fatherhood.
>
> (Beveridge 1906:327)

Emigration and labour colonies

Such ideologies were to have an important influence on the development of policies on and state support for birth control and sterilisation, in particular of working class and more recently of black women. As a response to the problem of unemployment over the turn of the century, however, they were to find their closest expression in the encouragement of emigration and of labour colonies.

The proposal of 'free' labour colonies for the rehabilitation of unemployed labour, and of penal labour colonies for the confinement of unemployable labour, was to gain considerable currency and official support. Usually established in rural areas – as was the first colony created by the Salvation Army at Hadleigh in Essex – they were seen as providing the vigour of the open air and the discipline of manual labour as a corrective to the debilitation of urban life (a perspective that was to continue in the 'treatment' of juvenile delinquency, many of the centres for which were subsequently established in premises originally set up as labour colonies). A number of such colonies were established, with the Local Government Board allowing poor relief to be paid in cash outside the workhouse to the dependants of any unemployed man willing to attend such a colony: a practice, with more than a shade of compulsion, that was to increase greatly in relation to the Labour Camps set up during the 1930s, and that continues to this day in government Re-Establishment Centres for the unemployed.

In practical terms, however, the creation of labour colonies to take the surplus of unemployed labour was not to get very far. Charles Booth's proposal, for example, for the 'entire removal' of his Class B 'out of the daily struggle for existence' (Booth 1904:154) would have meant the evacuation of some 345,000 people from London alone (Brown 1968). What was more significant, however, was the by now growing recognition that the unemployed were in fact not 'surplus' at all, but that they had a definite economic function as a reserve of labour. As Beveridge recognised by 1908.

The casual labourer of today is a part of industry, not outside industry. He cannot be regarded as unemployable so long as he is occasionally employed. He cannot be regarded as individually surplus since his services are occasionally in demand ...

The removal of the under-employed, whether to Canada, or to rural England, or to permanent national workshops, may benefit the men removed, but leave their places to attract and be filled by fresh comers.

(Beveridge 1908:387)

This recognition by certain social reformers of the economic functions and of the necessity of unemployment was to have profound implications for policy. More immediately, however, the fate of labour colonies as a viable solution to the problem of unemployment was to be sealed by a dramatic increase in unemployment that came with the slump in the economy following the end of the Boer War in 1902, and by a further increase in political protest and opposition.

By the autumn of 1904 the situation had become so serious that forty-five Poor Law Unions, twelve county councils and forty urban councils were to join forces with the trade union movement, the National Unemployed Committee that was set up by the Independent Labour Party, and even with the revolutionary Social Democratic Federation, to demand a special sitting of Parliament to deal with the crisis. The President of the Local Government Board later recalled:

It is all forgotten now, but during the eighteen months that the pressure of the unemployed was growing, the methods adopted by the unemployed towards all the authorities were violent in the extreme. There were crowds besieging the offices of the relieving officers – Boards of Guardians could hardly sit in some places without safeguarding their doors.

(Cited Brown 1971:44)

The Tory government, however, held out, unwilling to be seen to give way to pressure, and it was not until January 1905 that the Cabinet met to discuss the situation. At that meeting it considered proposals for emergency relief works, but faced with opposition from within its own ranks, from the C.O.S., and from the wealthy London boroughs which under the scheme would have had to contribute towards the cost of relief works in the poorer boroughs, the government prevaricated and delayed. By the summer it had done nothing when, on the 1st of August, serious rioting broke out in Manchester. Six days later a modified

version of the proposal had become law as the Unemployed
Workman Act.

The Unemployed Workman Act

The Unemployed Workman Act was to be the last major attempt
to deal with the problem of unemployment on an *ad hoc* basis. As a
scheme it drew its model entirely from the experience of the
previous twenty years; seeking to avoid criticism from the
C.O.S. and opposition from the wealthy London boroughs, the
scheme was to be initially financed entirely from voluntary
subscriptions. These were to be used to establish Distress
Committees – compulsory in London but optional elsewhere –
composed of local councillors, Poor Law guardians and 'persons
experienced in the relief of distress'. These Distress Committees
were to interview and investigate each applicant for assistance,
and:

> if satisfied that any such applicant is a person honestly
> desirous of obtaining work but unable to do so from excep-
> tional causes over which he has no control and that his case is
> capable of more suitable treatment under this Act than under
> the Poor Law ... [they may provide him with work] in such a
> manner as they think best calculated to put him in a position to
> obtain regular work or other means of supporting himself.
>
> (Cited Beveridge 1909:163)

As with the Chamberlain Circular of 1886, the Act sought to
provide relief work only for the 'deserving' unemployed temporarily out of work. As the Prime Minister later told the Royal
Commission on the Poor Laws:

> We distinctly proposed to deal with the *élite* of the unem-
> ployed ... The unemployed for whom the Bill was intended
> were respectable workmen settled in a locality, hitherto
> accustomed to regular work, but temporarily out of employ-
> ment through circumstances beyond their control, capable
> workmen, with hope of return to regular work after tiding
> over a period of temporary distress.
>
> (Report 1909 Vol I:493)

In the attempt to avoid what were seen as the failures of

previous relief works to discriminate between different forms of unemployment, and to exclude casual workers, the Distress Committees were given strict instructions of procedure to follow to test the character of applicants. According to Beveridge:

> The original 'Record Paper' drawn up by the Local Government Board contained eighteen paragraphs including at least fifty different questions to be asked of and answered by every applicant, together with six or more paragraphs for information to be entered after subsequent inquiry ... The answers to the most important questions were directed to be verified by reference to independent sources of information.
>
> (Beveridge 1909:24)

The Act was a mass of inquiry and investigation; in the words of Keir Hardie, 'every line had C.O.S. stamped across its face' (cited Harris 1972:174), for although the C.O.S. had initially opposed legislation on principle, once the government's intention to legislate became clear the C.O.S. had decided to throw its weight behind the scheme in order to secure its administration according to its own practice and philosophy. As a result, the scheme was not only cumbersome and expensive in its administration (in its first year, for every £35 spent in wages for relief work, £25 was spent in administration), but its emphasis on inquiring into character alienated the very workers it had intended to reach. As one contemporary observed, 'many of the best of the unemployed, especially skilled trade unionists, shun the Distress Committees' (Alden 1908:18).

Within the working class the Act was hailed by some as a victory, although the claim was a slender one. According to Hardie:

> The Unemployed Act was a small thing to have achieved, but it was the first blood which the Socialist party had drawn, for it established the principle that a man out of work had a claim upon the State to find employment for him.
>
> (Cited Gates 1910:5)

Such claims of a Right to Work were strenuously denied (see Churchill 1969:1054), but the creation of statutory relief works, particularly when carried only under pressure from the unemployed was seen by some as 'the surrender of a vital principle ...'

The Act has been defended on the ground that it is 'only a little one'; but it must be remembered that in poor-law administration a door which is partly opened is soon forced open to its widest extent, and that the Act has opened a door which has been closed for more than 70 years.

(Bailward 1907:72)

Nevertheless if a 'victory for the workers', it was only to be a partial one. Certainly, the payments made for relief work were to be at full trade union wage rates, although, like the Community Programme operated by the Manpower Services Commission, the authorities insisted that in order to maintain less eligibility the number of hours of relief work given had to be less than the hours worked in private employment. More significantly, and like much other social welfare legislation, while working class pressure may have been vital in securing change, it exerted very little influence over the form, content and administration of the reforms introduced, which as a result were able to continue to discriminate between and stigmatise the unemployed.

In many ways the Unemployed Workman Act marked a turning-point in the development of social reform: one of the last acts of an outgoing Conservative administration, its immediate, if reluctant, response to the threat of unemployment and social disorder through the creation of emergency relief works, its reliance on voluntary funding, and its particular concern with London to the neglect of other areas, all mark it in contrast to the planned and national system of Labour Exchanges, National Health and Unemployment Insurance that were to be the response of the new Liberal government that succeeded it in office.

Liberalism and social reform

Liberalism is a philosophy of the bourgeoisie, and just as the needs and interests of that class have changed over time, so too has the philosophy of liberalism. It was in the name of 'economic liberalism' that Adam Smith and other political economists had called for the setting-free of market forces at the beginning of the nineteenth century. At that time the philosophy of liberalism had been the cutting edge of capitalism in its struggle for

economic and political ascendancy. In similar vein, the Conservative Party that came to power in 1979 was to hark back to such
principles in its attempt to restore what it saw as the lost primacy
of market forces over economic and social life. As an editorial in
The Times in July 1977, aptly though misleadingly entitled 'Man is
Born Free', noted in relation to a speech by the future Prime
Minister:

> Mrs Thatcher is commonly regarded as belonging to the right,
> but this is because her belief in liberal economics is nowadays
> labelled right wing. In the past liberal economic theory has
> normally been regarded as a left wing cause... This belief,
> whose roots in history go back to the Middle Ages, has until
> very recent times been the underlying principle of those who
> wished to change British society rather than those who
> wished to preserve it in its existing form... Can it really be
> that this ideology of individualism... has suddenly become a
> reactionary influence, an obsolete idea?... What is certain is
> that they are ideas of revolutionary force... They dethroned
> King Charles I in England... They inspired the capture of
> power from the landowners by the middle class in the first half
> of the nineteenth century, and they inspired the great social
> reforms of the Liberal Party.

Ideas can indeed be a revolutionary force, but the ideology of
liberalism remained revolutionary only so long as it had a task to
do in overthrowing a feudal society and establishing capitalism as
the dominant mode of production; thereafter it was to become a
force for reaction and a means of preserving capitalism in the face
of the challenge of socialism.

Faced with this challenge, however, liberalism was also to
change. The old liberalism had posited a natural identity between
the classes and had embodied a view of society where the only
role for the state was that of removing artificial obstructions to
the operation of the market, so that prosperity and social
harmony could flow unaided. The 'new' liberalism that was
forged over the turn of the century, however, facing as it did
depression, stagnation and conflict, was to argue for a new
organic view of capitalism: a view of society in which individuals
were mutually interdependent, with certain rights and obligations – a reciprocity and stability, moreover, that could not be

expected to arise spontaneously out of the operation of market forces, but which had to be encouraged by and embodied in the state.

The state was to become the new cement of social unity. The resistance to state intervention that characterised the ideology of the ruling class was to be overturned. As Winston Churchill, one of the leading politicians of the new liberalism argued:

> I do not agree with those who say that every man must look after himself, and that intervention by the State in such matters ... will be fatal to his self-reliance, his foresight and his thrift ... It is a mistake to suppose that thrift is caused only by fear; it springs from hope as well as fear. Where there is no hope, be sure there will be no thrift.
>
> (Churchill 1909:209)

The fundamental tenets of capitalist ideology – the freedom of wage labour, the centrality of the market, the emphasis on thrift and self-help – were thus not to be discarded. Rather, in addition to, though not replacing the discipline of fear was to be added the incentive of hope: the fostering of a belief in and identification with the possibilities of a reformed capitalism in which the state would engage in social reform and partially lift the burdens of poverty and unemployment.

In part the new liberalism saw as its mission the mobilisation and education of its own class. In the pursuit of immediate profit, the owners of wealth had neglected the moral and political consequences of their actions. The result had been overproduction and unemployment, inefficiency, labour unrest and dissatisfaction, and the growth of a socialist movement within the working class that threatened to overthrow the entire structure. 'The master thought by which my politics are governed', wrote Mathew Arnold, 'is the thought of the bad civilisation of the English middle class' and the task of the new liberalism was 'to reproach them, though kindly, and mildly, for having made St Helens and places like it and exhort them to civilise themselves' (Arnold 1880).

The future of liberalism, as of capitalism, did not, however, lie solely in reforming the behaviour and attitudes of the bourgeoisie. The far greater threat came from the working class itself. If the threat of socialism was to be averted, means had to be found of securing working class loyalty and commitment to the status quo. In this task the new liberalism was to seek to identify itself with the workers' cause: 'the fortunes of Liberalism and Labour are inseparably interwoven', argued Churchill, 'they rise by the same forces, and in spite of similar obstacles, they face the same enemies' (Churchill 1909:71). This identification with labour, at times to the point of encouraging working class protest and discontent, was to serve two purposes. On the one hand it was to seek to outflank and undermine the appeal of socialism. On the other it was to attempt to ride the wave of working class discontent and use it to threaten the bourgeoisie into a recognition of the necessity for social reform. As one historian described one of the leaders of the new liberalism:

> Lloyd George simply stood for a policy of reform and concession by the employing class to meet the demands of labour to the extent necessary to avoid social upheaval and preserve national power... In this task, revolutionary class oratory, frightening to employers, consoling and diversionary to their workers, played a decisive role.
>
> (Adams 1953:61)

Or as Lenin saw him:

> A first class bourgeois businessman and master of political cunning, a popular orator, able to make any kind of speech, even revolutionary speeches before Labour audiences, capable of securing fairly consistent sops for the obedient workers in the shape of social reforms... Lloyd George serves the bourgeoisie splendidly. He serves it precisely among the workers, he transmits his influence to the proletariat, where it is most necessary and most difficult morally to subjugate the masses.
>
> (Cited ibid:64)

The role of the Labour Party

In 1906, following the defeat of the Tory government in the general election, the Liberal Party under the leadership of Campbell-Bannerman assumed office. One of its first acts was to appoint John Burns, previously a member of the revolutionary Social Democratic Federation and leader of the dockworkers' union, as President of the Local Government Board, with full responsibility for the Poor Law and the relief of unemployment.

Such action, while it raised alarm in many quarters, did not come as a surprise to all. As his former colleagues in the Battersea Branch of the SDF put it, it was 'the crowning act and the reward of a whole series of betrayals of the class to which he belonged' (cited Brown 1971:70). Burns had indeed already shown his predisposition for the post; as he told the Labour Representation Committee in 1900:

> I am getting tired of working class boots, working class trains, working class houses, and working class margarine. I believe the time has arrived in the history of the Labour and social movement when we should not be prisoners to class prejudice, but should consider parties and policies apart from all class legislation.
>
> (Cited Morton & Tate 1956:215)

Since the 1870s the Liberal Party had demonstrated its willingness to ally itself with sections of the labour movement, entering into a pact with some of the larger and more conservative trade unions, for whom it secured a degree of political representation and through which it sought to influence and moderate the temper of labour. By the early 1900s, however, Liberal attempts to contain working class politics were fast losing ground.

The formation of the Labour Representation Committee by a number of trades unions, socialist organisations and trades councils to press for independent working class representation in Parliament achieved its aim when in the 1906 election – from an electorate that was still confined to less than 20 per cent of the adult population – twenty-nine M.P.s were returned to form a distinct and separate Labour Party.

The arrival of the Labour Party was sufficient to fill sections of the ruling class, including many 'moderate' Liberals, with alarm. Not all, however, viewed its advent with such foreboding. As the *Independent Review*, the magazine of the growing radical wing of the new liberalism, saw it:

> We heartily welcome the new Labour Party which is now to make its first bow to the House of Commons... It will be a gain to the cause of social reform, since no pressure from

within the Liberal Party could prove so strong as the appearance of the Labour Party ... We cannot suppress a smile when noticing the alarm caused in a section of our press by the victory of the workers. The latter are asserting that the rich are now confronted with grave peril ... We hold a different opinion. Probably no less than twenty-three of the twenty-nine new M.P.s will call themselves socialists. But their socialism is rather an ideal, a point of view, than a programme of action.

> (Cited Rothstein 1929:289)

The socialism of the Labour Party, or at least of its Parliamentary leadership, was reformist: it sought not to overthrow capitalism, but to change it gradually from within. It was this acceptance of the legality of a capitalist state and its willingness to work within it that for the new liberalism made the Labour Party a welcome ally against the more threatening forms of revolutionary socialism. Considerably influenced by Fabianism, the Labour Party dismissed class conflict as a fundamental aspect of economic and social life, and instead portrayed itself as representing a 'national' interest. According to its first leader, Ramsay McDonald:

The future of the Labour Party is to be determined by its success in making its principles clear to itself and the country. If it narrows itself to a class movement, or a trade movement, or a manual workers movement ... it will weaken and finally disappear ... These conclusions are reached, not by a process of economic reasoning, or of working class experience. They rest upon conceptions of right and wrong common to all classes.

> (Cited Rothstein 1929:290)

The problems of poverty and unemployment were not, of course, moral issues, based on 'conceptions of right and wrong common to all', but problems based on fundamental and structural inequalities of wealth and power which no amount of moral consensus could hope to confront. At the same time, while the Labour Party claimed to represent a national interest, the basis of its support, even within the working class, was limited. Partly as a result of its foundation from within the largely male organised working class and trade union movement, and partly from its desire to establish its respectability amongst an electorate from which most of the working class was excluded, its attitudes towards the unorganised, towards women and towards the poor was, and has ever since remained, at best ambiguous. As Ramsay MacDonald put it, the Labour Party would 'never willingly touch a slum population or one that has shown no signs of intelligent initiative' (cited Jones 1975:34).

Even within the organised working class support for the Labour Party was contested by organisations, such as the SDF, which saw its policies and politics as insufficiently radical, and by those who fundamentally distrusted the lure of Parliamentary reform. Working class experience of the state, made many sceptical of the possibility of reforming capitalism beyond the achievement of a few palliative changes. As we shall see, the dilemma of reformism – the choice between accepting or rejecting piecemeal reforms that not only failed to challenge the underlying causes of poverty, but also weakened the struggle for more fundamental change – was to create major divisions within the working class and labour movement.

In the short term, however, the expectations raised by the formation of the Labour Party, and of the possibility of its influencing the new Liberal government to take decisive action on unemployment, were quickly to be disappointed. In its first year of office, the government did nothing other than to extend the operation of the Unemployed Workman Act, and when the Labour Party, under increasing pressure, put forward a Right to Work Bill its defeat by the government served only to increase disillusionment. In two by-elections in 1907 the complicity between the Labour and Liberal Parties were openly confronted. In Jarrow the Independent Labour Party secured the return of its own candidate against the wishes of the Liberals, while in Colne in Lancashire Victor Grayson, an independent socialist, was returned in opposition not only to the Liberals but also to the Labour Party itself.

Evidence of an increasingly radical shift within the working class was to provoke intense anxiety within the government. Following the two by-elections Sidney Buxton went to see John Burns at the Local Government Board to discuss the state of unemployment, but reported that he was able 'to extract nothing, except that "all is going well", which it is not' (cited

Brown 1971:603). The need to take more decisive action was growing, but as yet no substantial scheme of reform had been worked out.

Two forms of imperialism

The consequences of unemployment and poverty had high-lighted the need for social reform as a means of securing greater economic efficiency to service the ambitions of British imperialism. But the obstacles to British imperialism were more than just ones of economic inefficiency. As Semmel has argued:

> The main body of English socialism was not Marxist, but it was internationalist ... The suspicion that the growing social-ist working class would prove untrustworthy in an interna-tional conflict was widespread amongst the middle class.
>
> (Semmel 1960:22)

Over the opening decades of the twentieth century, the linking of eugenics and social Darwinism to portray other nations and unwillingness of British workers to lay down their lives in fighting the working class of other countries in order to secure the interests of British capitalism.

In this task, appeals to patriotism and jingoism were to be part of an ideology of nationalism that built upon popularised forms of eugenics and social darwinism to portray other nations and races as intrinsically inferior. Racism, however, has more than just an ideological foundation. The promise of increased living standards for the British working class that would arise from the exploitation by British capital of its overseas empire would come to provide an essential material basis for working class racism and an assault on its internationalism.

British imperialism, however, was also to be characterised by a fundamental division within the ruling class itself, between the interests of industrial and finance capital. Over the turn of the century both of these factions were to propose schemes of social reform in the attempt to win support for their own forms of imperialism.

Conflicts within the ruling class – whether between the inter-ests of agriculture and manufacturing, small-scale capital and large-scale capital, or industry and finance – are a constant source of tension, conflict and development. The Great Depression had revealed one such split: out of it the power of the City of London, of British finance capital, was to emerge relatively unscathed to maintain its position as the world's leading banker and financier. British industry, on the other hand, and especially the newer sectors which faced the greater competition from Germany, Japan and the United States, found itself in a much weaker position, excluded by tariff barriers from markets in the industrialising world and unable to maintain the levels of investment and profitability of its competitors.

It was in response to this situation that representatives of the iron, steel, glass and other industries, led by Joseph Chamberlain, the Birmingham screw manufacturer, met to form a movement for Tariff Reform. Over 53 million leaflets, pamphlets and posters were distributed on its behalf arguing for the creation of tariff barriers around the British Empire to exclude foreign goods and protect the jobs of British workers. As the owner of one national newspaper recalled:

> Joseph Chamberlain said to me one day: 'If you can only make working men understand that tariffs will give them work, you will have done the trick'. I then invented the famous slogan 'Tariff Reform Means Work For All'. We flaunted it day after day, week after week, on the front page of the Daily Express.
> (Cited Semmel 1960:112)

It was the Tory Party, to which Chamberlain had defected from the Liberal Party, that was to become the political champion of Tariff Reform. Finance capital, on the other hand, had other allies. As Lloyd George remarked of Lord Rothschild, 'you dare not mention this great potentate on a Liberal platform except in the language of idolatory' (Lloyd George 1910:9). The Liberal Party was to take up the campaign for Free Trade: for a form of imperialism which resisted the imposition of tariffs and which argued for a system of open world trade in which British capital could invest wherever the returns were greatest. As Lloyd George argued:

> We are a country that depends more upon its international trade than any other country in the world ... We carry for the whole world, and if we destroy our carrying trade we destroy our whole business. We cannot compare this country with

Germany (i.e. protectionism). We are the carriers of the world, the bankers of the world. We are the merchants of the world.
(ibid:8)

The appeal to the working class, however, could not be made solely on the basis of the financial prowess of the City of London. As the Liberal newspaper, the *Daily News* warned, 'the only conceivable and lasting destroyer of the policy of Mr Chamberlain is an alert and determined policy of social reform' (cited Harris 1972:212). Liberalism and Free Trade was in part able to find support in working class internationalism. It was also to promise cheaper food. As Winston Churchill was to argue with the radical oratory that typified the new liberalism:

Tariff reformers have declared that they will immediately proceed to put a tax on bread, a tax on meat, a tax on timber, and an innumerable schedule of taxes on all manufactured articles imported into the United Kingdom; that is to say, that they will rake by all these taxes a large sum from the pockets of the wage earners ... and that a great part of this large sum will be divided between the landlords and the manufacturers in the shape of increased profits.
(Churchill 1909:230)

Or as Lloyd George put it, 'if unemployment comes here it comes at any rate where food is cheaper, if it comes to protectionist countries it comes where food is dearest and most inaccessible to the workingman' (Lloyd George 1910:7).

Not only was 'protectionism ... bringing black bread to Germany' (ibid:16), but the advocates of Free Trade pointed to the similarly high levels of unemployment in both Germany and the United States to argue that tariff barriers were no solution to unemployment. Free Trade, on the other hand, or so it was argued, was essential to the protection of British jobs:

We have heard a good deal about capital being exported abroad ... but you have not seen capital exported abroad yet but that it comes back in orders for British goods ... If we do anything to impair our foreign trade we lose business, and how is that going to cure the problem of unemployment?
(Lloyd George 1910:4)

In such ways the two competing factions of capital were to

appeal for working class support in their differing policies of imperialism. When it came to social reform, however, the Liberal Party faced a more difficult issue, for the Tory Party could at least argue that the cost of social reform could be met from the proceeds of tariffs. As Asquith, who took over the Liberal leadership in 1908, pointed out:

> If it could not be proved that social reform (not socialism) can be financed on Free Trade lines, a return to protectionism is a moral certainty.
>
> (Cited Harris 1972:270)

As both parties recognised, the working class itself could not afford to bear alone the cost of old age pensions, the relief of sickness and unemployment, school meals or any other of the reforms that were promised. For the Liberals the answer was to lie in part in taxation of the rich. As Haldane, a leading Liberal, told Asquith:

> We should boldly take our stand on the facts and proclaim the policy of taking, mainly by direct taxation, such toll from the increase and growth of wealth as will enable us to provide for ... the increasing cost of social reform.
>
> (Cited Harris 1972:270)

The taxation of wealth was indeed a bold proposition but the new breed of Liberals were not noted for their temerity. Although the budget introduced by Lloyd George in 1910, with its proposals in particular for the taxation of land, was to be rejected by the House of Lords, and thus create a major constitutional crisis, the Liberal Party also was able to use such class divisions skilfully. The landed interest – the backbone of British capitalism until the beginning of the nineteenth century – was no longer the economic or political force it once was and, by tapping working class hostility towards the aristocracy in its rejection of 'The People's Budget', the Liberal government was able successfully to drive a wedge between the landed interest and the rest of the ruling class.

Moreover, the proposal to tax wealth, while radical, was itself justified as necessary to forestall an increasingly radical situation. As Haldane argued:

> The more boldly such a proposition is put the more attractive I

think it will prove. It will commend itself to many timid people as a bulwark against the Nationalisation of Wealth.

(Cited Harris 1972:270)

The threat of socialism, and of the total nationalisation of wealth, was to be used by the Liberals to convince their own class of the prudence of paying for social reform. As Churchill argued, they could well afford it: since 1900 the income tax assessment of the rich had increased by £109 million, the wages of the entire working class by only £10 million:

> You have therefore to choose between taking the millions which are needed for the defence of the realm and the social advance of the people from this great fund of capital, which has increased among its possessors to the extent of, on the average, £100 per head, on the one hand, or by going to the £1 per head which in the same period is all that has been secured by the wage earners.

(Churchill 1909:74)

It was they also who stood most to gain from its expenditure on social reform:

> The chief burden of the increase of taxation is placed upon the main body of the wealthy classes... That class has more to gain than any other class of His Majesty's subjects from dwelling amidst a healthy and contented people.

(ibid:291)

Socialism and social reform

Contentment was scarcely an accurate reflection of the state of feeling and opinion amongst the majority of the British population at the beginning of the twentieth century. Socialism, on the other hand, promised an alternative, and as disillusionment and hostility had grown, so the conditions of poverty and unemployment had come to be seen as themselves creating a breeding-ground for such a challenge.

It was in response to this threat, far outweighing the arguments for economic efficiency, that progressive social reformers came to see the necessity of social reform. Such reformers were not only to dismiss fears of the demoralising consequences of state intervention, but actively to promote state intervention as the only practicable means of overcoming working class hostility and of defusing the conflict that threatened. What this required was a fundamental change in the way that the state was presented to the mass of the population. As Sidney Webb put it:

> It seems desirable to promote in every way the feeling that 'the government' is no entity outside of ourselves, but merely ourselves organised for collective purposes. Regarding the State as a vast benefit society of which the whole body of citizens are necessarily members.
>
> (Webb 1890:104)

Or as Winston Churchill argued, there had to be '– at a low level – a sort of Germanized network of State intervention and regulation' (cited Gilbert 1966a:852).

Germany was a prime case in point. British capitalism's nearest and most threatening industrial and imperial competitor had also its own 'social problem': the home of Marx and Engels had also the most organised and militant working class in Europe. German capitalism also had the most sophisticated forms of defence. As the German Emperor argued in a speech to the Reichstag in 1881, referring back to the Anti-Socialist Law of 1878:

> A remedy cannot alone be sought in the repression of Socialistic excesses; there must be simultaneously the positive advancement of the welfare of the working classes. And here the care of those workpeople who are incapable of earning their livelihood is of the first importance.
>
> (Cited Dawson 1891:110)

By 1889 the German state had already established schemes for sickness, accident and old age insurance, and Germany was to become a mecca for British social reformers, politicians and civil servants who returned to marvel at its greater industrial and military efficiency and the political acumen of its leaders (see Braithwaite 1957). As one such observer, Harold Spender, put it:

> It is not enough for the social thinker in this country to meet the socialist with a negative. The English progressive will be

wise if, in this at any rate, he takes a leaf from the book of Bismarck, who dealt the heaviest blow against German socialism not by his laws of oppression... but by that great system of State insurance which now safeguards the German worker at almost every point in his industrial career.

(Cited Gilbert 1966b:257)

Social reformers recognised that while socialism and working class struggle could be, and indeed often was, met with repression, a more stable and long-lasting solution required that it be outflanked, and that this was a far wiser course, since 'those who are reformers cannot fail to recognise that the Socialists are touching a real grievance' (Arnold 1888:566). Recognising that there was 'a wide interval between rational social reform through legislation and socialism' (Lewis 1909:39), 'rational' reformers were to urge social reform as a means of undermining the appeal of socialism.

Of course there were then, as now, those amongst the ruling class that denounced such reforms as themselves 'socialistic'. But this was a label that many reformers such as Haldane were themselves willing, often eager, to accept:

If by socialism be meant the recognition that the time for reconstruction has come, and that the State must actively interfere in the process, then it is true we are all socialists.

(Cited Freedan 1972:7)

Or as another put it:

We are all socialists in the sense that our aim is the improvement of society. But there are socialists and Socialists... The socialists with a big 'S'... have proved immensely serviceable to the more rational body of reformers by forcing inquiry upon sluggish minds.

(Arnold 1888:560)

Bourgeois socialism was thus to be used in the battle against the socialism of the working class. As Marx and Engels explained, there was a fundamental difference; bourgeois socialism 'by no means understands abolition of the bourgeois relations of production... but administrative reforms, based on the continued existence of these relations; reforms, therefore, that in no respect affect the relations between capital and labour, but, at the best, lessen the cost and simplify the administrative work of bourgeois government' (Marx and Engels 1968:59). Or as one reformer confirmed:

> If we are all socialists now, as is so often said, it is not because we have undergone any change of principles of social legislation ... We are all socialists now only in feeling as much interest in these grievances as the Socialists are in the habit of doing, but we have not departed from our old lines of social policy, for they are broad enough to satisfy every claim of sound Social Reform.
>
> (Rae 1890:439)

The presentation of social reform as socialism has long been a major diversionary theme in the politics of social policy and in the history of the labour movement. Social reform and socialism are two fundamentally different projects, and while the former has often dressed itself up as the latter, in many instances social reform, as the Conservative leader Balfour put it in 1895, 'is not merely to be distinguished from socialism, but is its most direct opposite and its most effective antidote' (cited Halevy 1951:231).

For the Liberal Party the task, however, was 'to assimilate Socialism: if "liberalism" is not to become a mere shibboleth ... we must take from Socialism what is good and reject what is bad or doubtful' (*The Speaker*, cited Freedan 1972:46). In this task Liberalism found allies both in the Labour Party and in the state socialism of the Fabian Society. But its desire to harness working class socialism to the cause of social reform had to confront the ingrained and deep-rooted mistrust of and hostility towards capitalism and the state that had developed out of working class experience. For as George Holyoake, a leading figure in the working class co-operative movement, reminded them: 'State Socialism means the promise of a dinner, and a bullet when you clamour for it' (Holyoake 1878:510).

Social reform and the working class

Social reform is the product of class struggle; but this does not mean that social reforms reflect working class demands. On the contrary, while working class pressure has been decisive in determining the timing and scale of reform, the content and the control of social reform has most often been determined from within the ruling class. Social reform has more often served to undermine working class politicisation and pressure than to reflect it. As one Liberal social reformer noted:

> The present movement for social reform springs from above rather than below. The cry for an eight hours bill, for further factory legislation, for improvement of sanitation, for the re-adjustment of the incidence of taxation, for old age pensions, is less the spontaneous demand of the working classes than the tactical inducement of the political strategist.
> (Atherley-Jones 1893:629)

According to this view the success of social reform depended in part on its ability to win over at least a section of working class opinion and aspirations. As we shall see, there was a body within the working class that was amenable to such an inducement, and which was prepared to fight alongside social reformers for social amelioration. But for many, according to Henry Pelling (Pelling 1968:2), the promise of social reform was met either with opposition or disbelief. On the one hand there were those who simply saw through its piecemeal alterations:

> First, the normal working day of eight hours. We, as Socialists, of course condemn long hours, but the essential thing we condemn is the capitalist making a profit out of our labour at all. As long as this is done the hours of labour will really be regulated in the interest of the capitalist, not that of the community. It is the whole wages system that we contend against. Again, if the children are entitled to one free meal, they are entitled to all their meals free. We hold that they should be fed, clothed, sheltered and educated free by the community... Lastly as to taxes on large incomes. Under a proper system of society we should have no large incomes. It is possible that the governing classes will make a show of legislating in the direction of these palliatives; their doing so would certainly put off the revolution which we aim at. True Socialists, therefore, should not take up such catch cries.
> (Joseph Lane, cited Thompson 1957:126)

While such conscious and principled opposition existed amongst only a minority of the working class, far greater numbers of workers on the other hand were generally distrustful of the state, and hence of its offers of social reform. The bulk of such opposition was to come from the Friendly Societies and the Co-operative movement, but through them and other similar institutions, it was to be deeply ingrained within working class culture. As Thomas Hughes argued in his inaugural address as president of the Co-operative movement:

> We cannot repudiate the name 'socialist' in so far as it implies a belief that all human society is intended to be organised and will not be in its true condition until it is organised from top to bottom; but we have never looked to the state to do this for us.
> (Cited Youngjohns 1954:49)

It was this hostility towards the state – the identification of the state as belong to and serving the interests of an opposing class – that in the view of Joseph Chamberlain, who had been a leading advocate of a state old age pension, was 'the real ground of their resistance to my proposals . . . There is no doubt that this suspicion underlies the whole of the opposition . . . and this is the real and the true, and I might say the only reason which has led the officials, or some of the officials, of the Friendly Societies to offer resistance to my proposals' (Chamberlain 1892:607).

Finally there was that movement within the working class – both socialist and not – which believed that real and substantial gains could be made, and which criticised opposition to reform as impractical and divisive. It was to this section in particular that social reformers were to direct their patronage and encouragement. As one such organisation, the National Committee of Organised Labour for the Promotion of Old Age Pensions – an organisation founded by Charles Booth and funded largely by the Cadbury and Rowntree families – argued:

> A united demand for old age pensions on the part of organised labour would bring legislation at once . . . This is our own fault. We have cared more for political sects than for political principles . . . The true aim of the labour movement at this juncture is to concentrate its energies on certain leading ideas rather than dissipate them in pursuit of far-reaching theories

which may indeed be realised in the coming centuries but which do not belong to the work that lies nearest at hand.

(Cited Thane n.d.:6)

This of course was the great dilemma posed by reformism to an impoverished working class. Reform offered immediate improvement, however limited or partial it might be, while the achievement of socialism was a much more distant goal. It is a dilemma that has continued to haunt the labour movement. In 1944 Barbara Wootton posed the same problem in respect of the Beveridge Report:

> Somebody on the left is sure to be saying that the Beveridge Report is only tinkering with the problem, and that we should not be distracted by trivial piecemeal reform, but should concentrate all our energies on 'getting socialism first'... The Beveridge plan is *there*, ready to go on the statute books as it stands. I suggest that no one has a right to turn his back on it, in order to get socialism first, unless he has a plan for socialism which is equally ready to go into law at once – equally concrete, precise and detailed.

(Wootton 1944:12)

Socialism cannot be brought about through acts of legislation, no matter how detailed or precise; the overturning of existing social relationships, of the power of private property and the system of wage labour involves a much more fundamental transformation, and one which, moreover, requires the breaking of the power of the state. The fact that the revolutionary movement in Britain was insufficiently strong to create such a challenge meant that the lure of social reform was one that was difficult to refuse, even for those who saw through its intentions. As the Liverpool Trades Council argued in its annual report in 1894: 'Most of the council didn't like it at all... But when we saw the starvation and misery existing in our midst through lack of employment we considered it our duty to help and find some method of easing the suffering of our contemporaries' (cited Thane n.d.:7).

The limits of reformism, on the other hand, are often set by its inability to produce the goods. By 1908, despite the promises and despite the expectations raised within sections of the working class by the formation of the Labour Party, no new initiatives on unemployment had been taken. By June of 1908 registered unemployment had reached 8 per cent:

> Violence broke out in several cities. Windows were smashed in Manchester in protest against the government's inactivity, while in Glasgow workers from over forty trades took part in a massive anti-government demonstration... But working class discontent was not directed solely against the government, for many voices were raised against the apparent quiescence of the Labour Party.
>
> (Brown 1971:96)

It was this last point which for the ruling class was potentially the most threatening, for having guided and encouraged working class protest into parliamentary reform, there was, as another historian has noted, 'growing evidence that large numbers of workers were losing faith in the political method of making gains for labour' (Sires 1955:247). Disenchantment with the parliamentary process was confirmation of the claims of those revolutionary socialists who had argued that substantial reform was beyond the intent or capabilities of the capitalist state. This disenchantment was now to spill out onto the streets and into the factories in an unprecedented wave of political and industrial unrest.

On October 10th 1908 twenty separate hunger marches took place in London, and two days later Parliament was forced to reassemble, ringed by a cordon of two and a half thousand police. The same year, moreover, saw the beginnings, in a strike and subsequent lock-out in the textile industry, of a wave of industrial action that was to develop through many key industries into a movement of revolutionary syndicalism, rejecting parliamentary politics and advocating direct workers' control, and that was to bring the working class in a number of areas into confrontation with state troops. As Churchill told the Prime Minister in December:

> There is a tremendous policy in Social Organisation. The need is urgent and the moment ripe. Germany with its harder climate and far less accumulated wealth has managed to establish tolerable basic conditions for her people. She is organised not only for war, but also for peace. We are organised for nothing except party politics.
>
> (Cited Churchill 1969:865)

Administrative reform

Changes in state administration – the creation, for example, of the Manpower Services Commission in 1974 to take over responsibility for dealing with unemployment from the Department of Employment – often reflect much deeper shifts of politics and policy, as well as conflicts within the state apparatus itself. So it was at the beginning of the present century, when recognition of the need to do something about working class unemployment was to lead to a major shift of responsibility within the state machinery.

We have already seen how the relief works set up by the Chamberlain Circular and the Unemployed Workman Act were intended to provide for the so-called deserving unemployed outside of the operation of the Poor Law. When similarly the Board of Trade had begun in 1886 to collect statistics on unemployment, this signalled a move that was to be of increasing importance. In part the decision to by-pass the Local Government Board, which until then was the government agency with sole responsibility for the unemployed, arose from the fact that its information and statistics were, according to the President of the Royal Statistical Society, 'universally regarded as useless' (cited Davidson 1971:125). In part also, the decision of the Board of Trade to collect its own intelligence on unemployment was recognition of the seriousness with which the problem was viewed within the state, and the need for serious study and consideration. This was further confirmed in 1893 by the creation of a separate Labour Department within the Board of Trade, and the appointment as its senior civil servant of Sir Hubert Llewellyn Smith, a radical liberal social reformer who, according to his biographer, 'was immersed in the kaleidoscopic world of late Victorian progressivism' (Davidson 1971:17). Thereafter, according to Davidson:

> The Labour Department submitted regular reports upon the state of employment to the Cabinet, their objectivity standing in marked contrast to those of the Local Government Board which often consisted of reactionary diatribes against the unemployed.
>
> (Davidson 1971:129)

While such diatribes played (and continue to play) their part, effective state policy required a more informed approach. For this, the Local Government Board was ill-suited. As Haldane commented with respect to its President, appointed in 1906 in what had then been seen as a radical move:

> Burns, who had great oratorical gifts, but not much knowledge, was beginning to be out of date with labour. What was needed was a new and enlightened attitude to social problems.
>
> (Cited Caldwell 1959:377)

The need for an enlightened approach to the problem was not, however, to lead to the abolition of the Local Government Board and the Poor Law, or even their reformation. The system of poor relief based on stigma and deterrence was recognised as inhumane and distasteful, as too harsh for the 'deserving' unemployed, and as politically unstable, but it was not altogether irrelevant. While the development of policies for the 'deserving' unemployed was to become the responsibility of the Board of Trade, the Poor Law itself was to remain, and remain in the same stigmatising form, to deal with chronic poverty and unemployment, and to attempt to discipline and remoralise the casual and 'undeserving' poor.

The system of poor relief, whether in the form of the Poor Law, National Assistance, Supplementary Benefit or Income Support, has in many respects remained the pariah of the state welfare system. It is an institution from which other supposedly more enlightened departments of state, such as those involved in child care or health provision, have sought to distance themselves. In 1943, for example, the Minister of Health rejected proposals that Assistance Board officers should act as sick visitors in the investigation of claims for the new National Health Service, since 'it will be fatal to the conception of the health service if it becomes too much associated with the giving or withholding of cash benefits' (Public Record Office PIN 8/4). Yet at the same time it is an institution on which these other state departments have continued to depend, which deals with those people they cannot or will not deal with, and on whose performance as a residual and disciplinary mechanism, as the experiments in relief work had shown, they depend for their own viability.

In 1908 Campbell-Bannerman resigned as Liberal Prime Minister and was replaced by Asquith. By then it was clear that unemployment and the problems associated with it were not going to go away, and that, with accelerating industrial and political conflict, something decisive needed to be done. It was now that the new liberals were to take the lead. Previously restricted to argument and persuasion from outside the corridors of power, they were now to be given their head: in the Cabinet reshuffle that followed the change in Prime Ministers, Lloyd George was appointed as Chancellor of the Exchequer, with a special brief on health and national efficiency, and Winston Churchill, having been offered but having refused the Presidency of the Local Government Board, was appointed to the Board of Trade, 'only on the understanding that the unemployment question should now be tackled from this department' (cited Brown 1964:607). There he was to work with Llewellyn Smith and William Beveridge on a policy for unemployment.

Labour exchanges and the reserve army of labour

With politicians and reformers arguing that the distribution of income and wealth had to be left to the 'natural' play of economic forces, and thus the creation of depression and unemployment regarded as inevitable (see Beveridge 1909:63), attention was to focus on the forms which unemployment took and the consequences it had for economic and political stability. Of these forms, one of the most widespread and problematic was the existence of casual work as a means of maintaining a reserve army of labour.

As we have seen, casual labour was a means by which employers could maintain at hand a constant supply of under-employed workers in order to meet fluctuations in business and to resist claims for increased wages and prevent shop-floor organisation. Although many reformers viewed casual labour as itself the product of the character of the unemployed – a result of laziness or lack of discipline (see, for example, Beveridge 1909:144) – such strictures could offer no real solution to the problems of poverty and deterioration that characterised the casual labour system. As Beveridge also argued, it could not solely be 'explained away as the idleness of the unemployable . . .

it is too widespread and too enduring for that' (Beveridge 1908:386). Or as Churchill saw it:

> The casual labourer . . . whose whole life and the lives of his wife and children are embarked in a sort of blind, desperate, fatalistic gamble with circumstances beyond his comprehension or control . . . is not as a class the result of accident or chance, is not casual because he wishes to be casual . . . The casual labourer is here because he is wanted here. He is here in answer to a perfectly well-defined demand.
>
> (Churchill 1909:202)

This more radical and realistic appreciation of the causes and dynamics of casual labour was a necessary precondition for any effective solution to the problem. The solution, however, was not to lie in the abolition of casual labour. Although the state was to attempt to persuade employers to decasualise their workforces, and although the introduction of Wages Councils was to bring in minimum wage rates in a few selected occupations, it was widely recognised that, as Charles Booth put it, 'our modern system of industry will not work without some unemployed margin, some reserve of labour' (cited Hobson 1895:418). The problem was rather that the existing forms of maintaining this reserve were unable to prevent widespread poverty and disaffection:

> It is in essentials a problem of business organisation – that of providing a reserve of labour power to meet fluctuations in such a way as to not involve distress.
>
> (Beveridge 1909:110)

In part the problem of casual labour was seen as the practice of employers each to have their own casual labour force, resulting in a series of casual labour markets which taken together far exceeded employers' aggregate demand. For Beveridge, therefore, the answer was to lie in a national organisation of the labour market, and the creation of a system of Labour Exchanges which, he hoped, would:

> become the headquarters of a compact mobile reserve of labour, replacing and by its mobility covering the same ground

as the large reserve which drifts more slowly and blindly about the streets today.

(Beveridge 1909:203)

National Insurance

The creation of a national system of Labour Exchanges under the Board of Trade in 1908 was the first step towards a solution of the problem of unemployment: 'the only remedy consistent with the continuance of private enterprise for the most urgent and perplexing part of the unemployed problem' (Beveridge 1907:73). State organisation of the labour market, however, was to do little to solve the problem of the maintenance of those who remained or who would become unemployed. Here, as again we have already seen, the concern of social reformers about the consequences of unemployment did not extend to all of the unemployed. The need to maintain the pressure of poverty as a spur to wage labour meant that for many – for the unskilled, for casual workers or for the chronic poor and unemployed, all of whom competed for low-paid jobs at the bottom of the labour market – the pressures of poverty could not be removed. But for the more skilled and the more regularly employed, reasons both of economic efficiency and political stability demanded a more lenient treatment. As Beveridge had argued, in relieving distress:

the problem is not how to relieve all distress whatsoever ... A relief scheme is good or bad according as it does or does not, to the exclusion of all others, get hold of the right class of men, the men suffering from 'cyclical' depression of employment and does or does not preserve them through the depression to recover their places as soon as possible in regular industry ... It must concentrate itself upon the task of preserving the efficiency of those workers alone who are temporarily unemployed as the consequence of a periodic depression of trade.

(Beveridge 1904c:44)

Attempts to exclude the chronic poor and unemployed had, in the case of relief works, proved unworkable. In the light of that experience, according to Llewellyn Smith:

The crucial question from a practical point of view is therefore whether it is possible to devise a scheme which, while nominally covering unemployment due to all causes, shall automatically discriminate between classes of employment... [which] itself will automatically exclude the loafer.

(Cited Beveridge 1930:265)

The answer was to lie in 'Insurance. That is the future - insurance against dangers from abroad, insurance against dangers scarcely less grave and much more near and constant which threaten us here at home in our own island' (Churchill 1909:309).

National Insurance was to be the epitome of Liberal social democracy. Its provision of non-means tested benefit outside of the stigma and disenfranchisement of the Poor Law for the 'deserving' unemployed was to be the reward of good citizenship; its insistence on contributions not only from workers but also from employers and from the state was to symbolise a national unity, 'to revive the feeling of fellowship between capital and labour' (Lewis 1909:63), and to use the power of the state to force employers to take some responsibility for the problem; and its involvement of both the trade union movement and the Friendly Societies in its administration was to seek to incorporate working class institutions within the machinery of the state and, in Churchill's words, to 'so far demonstrate the complexity of the problem as to dispose finally of all rough and ready revolutionary solutions' (cited Harris 1972:365).

The National Insurance scheme itself came in two parts. The first, which established a system of sickness benefit payable to insured workers, was, according to Lloyd George, 'the foundation of national efficiency' (Lloyd George 1911:1). It was partly on this basis that he sought to justify the principle of the employers' contribution, since 'German experience shows that organised provision for the health of the working class produces increased efficiency... If, as I hope, these influences more than counterbalance the burden which we are asking employers to bear, the cost of production will be diminished rather than increased' (*The Times*, 12/5/1911). Moreover, it was widely recognised that such contributions, if required from all employers, would not detract from profitability, since the cost would be passed on in higher costs to the consumer; or, as Asquith put in bluntly: 'the blood of the workman is part of the cost of the product' (cited Searle 1971:63).

The principle of the workers' contribution was, however, concerned with more than just finance. For both the unemployment and health insurance schemes, the contributions paid have been no more than another form of taxation - transferring income from those in work to those out of work. Yet the earmarking of specific contributions from the workers' pay packets, rather than funding the scheme out of general taxation, was seen as vital. As Lloyd George explained:

> The greatest evil which has to be guarded against in all benefit schemes of this character comes from the danger of malingering... The most effective check, in fact the only really effective check, upon malingering is to be found in engaging the self-interest of the workmen themselves in opposition to it. That is why a purely state scheme would inevitably lead to unlimited shamming and deception. This scheme is so worked that the burden of mismanagement and maladministration would fall on the workmen themselves. If, through any cause, there is any deficiency, they must make it up either in diminished benefits or increased levies. Once they realise that, then malingering will become an unpopular vice amongst them.
> (Memo on the National Insurance Bill, Public Records Office, PIN 3/3, 1911)

Thus the insurance stamp was intended to make it clear to those in work how much the relief of unemployment or sickness was costing them, and to turn them against any generous treatment of the unemployed. The danger of 'malingering' was also to be dealt with in other ways. The Labour Exchanges already existed to ensure that 'you do not have a man who is not genuinely unemployed getting unemployment pay', but in addition:

> The scheme should avoid encouraging unemployment, and for this purpose it is essential that the rate of unemployment benefit should be relatively low.
> (Llewellyn Smith 1910:527)

The need to 'imply a sensible and even severe difference between being in work and out of work' (Churchill, cited Harris 1972:365) was to be expressed in a rate of benefit, both for unemployment and sickness, that has ever since been little, if at all, above the rate of statutory poor relief. The major difference, however, was that insurance benefits were paid without a means test and, subject to certain conditions, provided not at the discretion of relieving officers or officials, but as a right to those who qualified by way of contributions.

It was this principle of contributions which ensured that National Insurance automatically discriminated in favour of the deserving sick and unemployed. Only those who had previously been in regular employment, and who had thus built up a sufficient record of contributions, would be eligible for its benefits, while the chronic poor and unemployed, casual workers, most women and many of the unskilled would be excluded. Their destitution was to continue to be dealt with under the Poor Law and the workhouse, where, according to Balfour, they were to receive 'a stern lesson of the necessity of industry, self-exertion, self-reliance and self-respect' (cited Rodgers 1969:39).

Symbolic of this lesson was the penalty of disenfranchisement, for unlike the deserving poor who received insurance benefits, those who claimed poor relief lost the right to vote. As Beveridge explained:

> Many of the 'undeserving' unemployed, undeserving that is of anything better than a rigorous Poor Law, are voters, to whom it would be ruinous policy to allow electoral control over any public relief agency by which they hoped to bene-fit... Disenfranchisement is based upon two grounds. In the first place, men who cannot in ordinary circumstances support themselves in independence are not citizens in fact and should not be so in right; disenfranchisement in this view is part of the stigma of pauperism. In the second place it is dangerous to allow recipients of public relief to elect its dispensers.
>
> (Beveridge 1905:102)

Those who were in ordinary circumstances unable to support themselves were thus not to be considered citizens, were not to be part of the new social democracy, and were to be excluded from its benefits. For the remainder – largely the skilled, male organised working class – those who presented capitalism with its greatest political challenge, the extension of citizenship was to attempt to incorporate them within the existing structure of society and secure their attachment to the state. As Llewellyn

Smith shrewdly recognised, 'military discipline is right for the "submerged", but democracy is the only hope for labour in general' (cited Davidson 1971:227). Or as Churchill summed it up:

> The idea is to increase the stability of our institutions by giving the mass of industrial workers a direct interest in maintaining them. With a 'stake in the country' in the form of insurance against evil days, these workers will pay no attention to the vague promises of revolutionary socialism ... It will make him a better citizen, a more efficient worker, and a happier man.
>
> (Cited Harris 1972:365)

The limits of reform

The period between 1880 and 1914 was one of the most significant for the development of a welfare state in Britain, laying down the foundations for new developments in social policy, both in philosophy and practice, that were later to be extended in the period following the Second World War.

The significance of these developments was, however, to be more ideological than material. Although the 'new' Liberalism promised greater security, better provision and a more humanitarian state, the realities of capitalist production both demanded and resulted in a less neat and tidy picture. Thus the 'lure' of social reform was not to be wholly successful in buying off the discontent and opposition of the working class. Had more been on offer, it might – as other countries were later to discover – have indeed been more successful. But the over-riding fear of the British ruling class of being seen to give too much too readily to those they wished to keep in their place set the limits far short of what would have been necessary to lead workers to believe a new dawn was in the making. Class conflict was to continue and to intensify.

Neither did the benevolent humanitarianism of the state long outlast the second Great Depression that hit the world during the 1920s and 1930s. Here again a concern not to alienate the most organised and most powerful sections of workers was an important aspect of state policy, and led to further attempts at discrimination and new forms of relief. But such innovations lasted only as long as the political challenge which provoked them, and were withdrawn as soon as the situation would allow. The power of market forces and the willingness of governments to give way to them would, in the inter-war years, show up quite clearly the limits of reform.

In the final analysis, it was perhaps not so much Liberal social reforms which solved the problem of unemployment and of 'surplus' casual labour, but the carnage of the First World War. Thirty years later, after the world had seen a further forty million dead, the Second World War would again solve the problem of overproduction and create for capitalism a new shortage of labour. Seen in this light, and in the midst of the third Great Depression in the 1980s, the fragile balance of world peace begins to look frighteningly precarious. Wars, of course, do not just solve problems for capitalism, they also create other ones, and after the Second World War the advanced capitalist societies were to be faced with new sets of problems. In Britain these problems were to be responded to with further advances in welfare, but they were in the main advances within a structure and philosophy that had already been established at the beginning of the century.

part three

THE WELFARE STATE

five

THE RISE AND FALL OF SOCIAL DEMOCRACY

The politics of growth; the Beveridge 'revolution'; women and children last; social security and democracy; the elusiveness of power; maintaining the incentive to work; divide and rule; the impasse of social democracy.

> The peculiar character of the Social Democracy is epitomised in the fact that democratic–republic institutions are demanded as a means, not of doing away with two extremes, capital and wage labour, but of weakening their antagonism and transforming it into harmony.
>
> (Karl Marx *The Eighteenth Brumaire*)

The Labour government that came into office in 1945 was elected on a wave of popular and radical expectations. The mass mobilisation created by the Second World War, the increased strength of trades unions, the marked shift in the experiences and expectations of many working people, and in particular of women, and the example shown by the state of its ability to suspend market forces and successively engineer a more planned and ordered economy, all had contributed to turn the war into a struggle for a better society in Britain as well (see Calder 1971). The determination that there should be no return to the mass poverty and unemployment of the 1930s saw the humiliating defeat of the national war hero, Winston Churchill, and the victory of a Labour government with the largest majority in parliamentary history. As its members rose to sing the Red Flag in the hallowed House of Commons it seemed, to some, that the world had finally been turned upside down (see Gallacher 1951).

Just over thirty years later another Labour government, led by James Callaghan, was to suffer a similarly humiliating defeat at the hands of a new Conservative administration. The triumph of the Thatcher government in 1979, however, marked more than just another swing in the political see-saw between Conservative and Labour governments in Britain that had characterised the post-war years. Thatcherism, as it quickly came to be known, represented a radical departure not only from previous Labour administrations, but also from those of post-war Conservative governments. It deliberately challenged the post-war consensus that had existed between the political parties and set out consciously to attack both the principles and the practice of state welfare provision.

Between the events of 1945 and 1979 lie a great many events and circumstances which go towards an explanation of this remarkable reversal in British politics. Many of these, such as the record of betrayals, divisions and splits within the Labour Party, though important, are themselves secondary reflections of a more basic series of conflicts and problems. Underlying them is the experience of social democracy itself: of a form of politics most closely associated with the Labour Party, although shared to a greater or lesser extent by alternating Conservative governments until 1979. It is a form of politics which sought to reconcile the conflicting interests of capital and labour, which used the power of the state in the attempt to maintain social harmony, but which left the fundamental structures and institutions of capitalism intact. In short, it was a form of politics which, as Alexander Campbell had argued in 1842, 'merely changed the form of government without changing the form of society', and which, as he had predicted, 'begins in delusion and ends in disappointment' (cited Youngjohns 1954:26).

The politics of growth

The post-war settlement between capital and labour was predicated on economic growth. For nearly thirty years the world's capitalist economies grew at an unprecedented and more or less steady rate. Led by the United States, fuelled by the growth of the permanent arms economy and mass consumerism and sustained by imperialism, with its subjugation of the Third World to the benefit of the advanced economies, the post-war boom created the opportunity for a sustained rise in working class standards of living.

In Britain the boom served to obscure, at least for a time, the country's outmoded and declining industrial base. Having entered the process of industrialisation earlier than its main competitors, and thereafter failing to reinvest domestically in new plant and machinery at a comparable rate, its underlying level of productivity was to slip behind that of countries like Germany or Japan. As a consequence, when the boom began to falter in the late 1960s and early 1970s, the impact on the British economy was to be that much more severe. In the meantime, however, the advantages gained by its colonial legacy and the continued growth and strength of finance capital allowed the British economy to ride the boom with considerable success.

For nearly thirty years unemployment in Britain averaged around and often less than 2 per cent, and much of that was accounted for by workers moving between different jobs. A growing demand for labour, boosted by the shortage created by the war itself as well as by post-war reconstruction, inevitably led to higher levels of economic and social mobility. New jobs were created, for example in the white collar supervisory and technical fields, or in the professions of an expanding state welfare system, and the middle class grew in numbers and proportion. Within the working class, economic expansion also allowed, for some, an upward mobility, into more skilled jobs, with higher levels of security and pay.

As the largest single employer, and with an increasing proportion of the gross national product passing through its hands, the state played an important part in maintaining economic stability and growth. The once familiar cycle of boom and slump all but disappeared as successive Labour and Conservative governments used what controls they had over the economy to iron-out fluctuations and maintain relatively full employment. For a significant proportion of workers (especially those who were white, male and skilled) the post-war boom meant, for the first time, a degree of economic security and the prospect of a steady and continuous rise in standards of living.

From the point of view of capital the boom, while it created the opportunity for making money, also created many problems. First and foremost amongst these was that sustained economic growth created a relative shortage of labour, and in doing so threatened to shift the balance of power in bargaining over wages and conditions in favour of workers. Various measures were employed in the attempt to keep this tendency in check, one of the most significant of which was the search for new reserves of labour to fill the vacuum.

During the 1950s in particular both private employers and the state combined to search out fresh reserves of labour from abroad. Recruiting offices were set up in the West Indies, Pakistan and India to encourage the migration of black workers to work in the lower-paid jobs left by their white counterparts. In public transport, parts of the textile and iron industries as well as in the hospital services, black workers were recruited to do the 'dirty work' and the anti-social shifts, at rates of pay consistently lower than those of the rest of the population. The use of such workers as cheap labour was compounded, and in many respects made possible, by the existence of racism. Faced with discrimination in both the private and public housing markets and in the labour market, black workers found themselves ghettoised both in places of work and in places to live. At best neglected by the trade union movement, and at worst subject to racist abuse and attacks, the rejection of black workers by much of the white community served to reinforce their isolation and exploitation (see, eg, Fryer 1984; Castles 1984).

The other major source of labour to which employers looked to fill the gap was that of women, and in particular of married women, who before the Second World War had constituted only 10 per cent of the workforce. By 1951 21 per cent of married women were working, in 1961 32 per cent and by 1972 47 per cent. Many married women had, of course, working during the war, and in a wide range of occupations. What was different during the post-war years was both that women's work was largely restricted to unskilled and/or predominantly 'female occupations', and that the facilities such as day nurseries which the state had provided during the war to facilitate women's entry into the labour market were rapidly eroded (see Wilson 1980). The participation of married women in the labour market during the post-war boom therefore took placed under a growing 'double burden' of low-paid waged work and unpaid domestic work: a burden that was made all the more heavy by a body of academic writing, often enshrined in state welfare policies, which warned of the dangers of 'latch-key children' and the psychological damage caused by separation from their mothers. Again, women were a growing part of the labour force largely neglected by the male-dominated trade union movement. Just as racism served to divide the labour movement, and enable the use of black workers as cheap labour, so too sexism, with its belief that women worked only for pin money, that their jobs were not as important as those of men, and that their proper place was in the home enabled capital to take advantage of a more or less captive source of low-paid unorganised workers.

The employment of black workers and of women provided capital with a lever to offset the potentially disruptive effect of full employment on wage levels and factory discipline. The relative neglect of racism and sexism by the organised labour movement, both in the form of the trades unions and of the Labour Party and its government, and at the worst, their active endorsement of racist and sexist practices and legislation, for example on immigration control, played a large part in allowing such divisions to be perpetuated. Social democracy was very much the politics of a white male working class, and although it was to come under increasing pressure from women and from black workers, its response, such as at Grunwick, was more often symbolic than sustained.

Pressure on capital nevertheless remained, and here again the state, acting in the so-called 'national interest', was to play an important part in attempting to regulate the pace of growth and restrain working class demands. From the 'stop-go' policies of the 1950s to the incomes policies and social contract of the 1970s successive governments tried to put a brake on the new-found security and strength of labour.

The post-war establishment of the welfare state was part of this struggle and compromise, and its expansion over the following decades reflected the precarious state of the balance of class and other social forces. It was not, just as social policy has never been, simply a case of capitalism giving concessions to a more organised and demanding working class. When Quintin Hogg warned the House of Commons in 1945: 'If you do not give the people social reform, they are going to give you social revolution', he was reflecting an important theme in the development of social welfare, echoing Chamberlain's famous question over fifty years earlier when he said 'I ask what ransom property will pay for the security it now enjoys'. But welfare has never been simply a case of 'buying-off' discontent. It has certainly attempted to do that, but it has also been an important mechanism for defusing class conflict, for creating and reinforcing divisions amongst the poor and within the working class, for buttressing the unequal operation of the labour market, and for sustaining those ideologies – about poverty, the role of women, or about work incentives – on which the successful operation of capitalism has depended.

In this respect the welfare state is not an homogeneous entity. There are elements within it that can be viewed as progressive, as representing the values of collectivism and equality against the values of individualism and inequality. There are parts of it which are liberating and parts that are repressive and coercive. What balance is struck between the two extremes has depended historically on the balance of class forces, as well as other forms of political struggle, just as it has also depended upon the particular problems or groups within the population to which policies have been addressed. Thus, for example, within Britain the National Health Service has often been seen as the 'jewel' of the welfare state, and popularly defended as its most significant achievement. This is itself a reflection of a variety of factors: the power of the medical profession, the willingness of capital to see a 'socialisation' of medical care in the interests of greater efficiency, the popular demand for provision on the basis of need rather than ability to pay, as well as its defence by a powerful and vocal middle class who have in many respects been its main beneficiaries. That parts of the welfare state have been of greater advantage to the better-off than to the poor is true also in the case of the education system, whose inequalities mirror the society it serves. The further, however, that welfare provision moves away from a 'universal' provision, and the closer it gets to dealing with the fundamental issues of inequality, of poverty and the labour market, in general the more punitive, stigmatising and constrained it becomes.

The Beveridge 'revolution'

The Beveridge Report, published in 1942, remains the symbol of the arrival of the welfare state in Britain. It was not, however, a revolution; unless, that is, we accept Marx's observation on the succession of bourgeois revolutions in nineteenth-century France where

> in its struggle against the revolution, the parliamentary republic found itself compelled to strengthen along with the repressive measures, the resources and centralisation of governmental power. All revolutions perfected this machine instead of smashing it.
>
> (Marx and Engels 1968:169)

The Beveridge Report and its subsequent legislation did not seek to overthrow pre-existing structures and relationships. As Beveridge himself argued: 'the scheme proposed here is in some ways a revolution, but in more important ways it is a natural development from the past. It is a British revolution' (HMSO 1942: para.31). This 'British revolution' was indeed to strengthen and perfect the machinery of governmental power, and was to do so in ways which built upon principles and practices developed from the past. Certainly there were innovations – the introduction of family allowances and maternity benefits, for example, or the more far-reaching proposals, which although strictly outside of the terms of the Beveridge Report were closely associated with it, for the creation of a National Health Service and a government commitment to full employment – but the essential principles, structures and administration of social security which emerged from the post-war legislation were fundamentally unchanged. It was a major reform, but not a revolution.

This is not to deny that the Report was presented as marking a revolutionary change in social policy, nor that it was seen as such by much of the labour movement and by at least some sections of the ruling class (although as Sir John Walley, Deputy Permanent Secretary in the Ministry of Pensions and National Insurance, pointed out, 'the basic ideas in the Beveridge Report could hardly have surprised anyone versed in current thinking about social security in the 1920s' (Walley 1972:40)). The vast amount of governmental and non-governmental publicity and

propaganda which greeted its publication – a propaganda campaign that was seen as essential in maintaining working class
commitment to the war effort – heralded the Report as marking
the beginning of a new future, as the expression of a new
democracy and a 'post-capitalist' society in which poverty and
unemployment would be finally and irrevocably abolished and in
which the state would assume full responsibility for the welfare
of its citizens 'from the cradle to the grave'. The reality was to be
somewhat different.

The basis for this coverage was to be a system of universal
social insurance. Created in 1911, the system of National
Insurance provided unemployment benefit for a relatively small
group of largely male workers in a number of key occupations,
and a more widespread system of sickness benefit based on
contributions. By 1920 the scope of the Unemployment
Insurance scheme had been widened to include all full-time
manual workers, although significantly large occupational
groups such as those in agriculture or in domestic service
remained excluded. The Beveridge Report proposed the compulsory extension of the National Insurance system for both
sickness and unemployment to all full-time workers, with the
exclusion of married women. These benefits, as previously, were
to be dependent on contributions, since according to the Report
(although there was no evidence to support the view) this 'is
what the people of Britain desire' (HMSO 1942: para.21). What
was significantly new in the Report, and what was importantly to
be omitted in the subsequent legislation, were the proposals
firstly that the benefits paid should last for as long as sickness or
unemployment persisted, and secondly that the level of benefit
should be sufficient to maintain those dependent on it above the
poverty line without further assistance.

The contribution principle that lay at the heart of the
Beveridge proposals was thus not new. It already existed in
unemployment and sickness benefit, and had been introduced as
a principle for determining entitlement to old age pensions when
the previous non-contributory scheme was replaced in 1929. As
a principle for determining entitlement to benefit, it was
seriously flawed, for whilst Beveridge's vision had been of a
society in which, as a result of full employment, all workers
would find themselves covered by the insurance scheme, the

reality of the post-war labour market was such that a significantly large and growing proportion of the workforce would find
themselves excluded from the scheme. The system of flat-rate
contributions proposed in the Report was also highly regressive;
even with the introduction of earnings-related contributions in
1966, National Insurance payments are a form of taxation which
fall proportionately most heavily on the lowest paid. Beveridge
himself was conscious and deliberately intended that his scheme
should not attempt to solve the problem of poverty by redistri-
buting resources from rich to poor. As he argued in his Report:

> Abolition of want cannot be brought about merely by increas-
> ing production without seeing to correct distribution of the
> product. But correct distribution of the product does not mean
> what it has often been taken to mean in the past: distribution
> between land, capital, management, and labour. Better distri-
> bution is required among wage earners themselves, as
> between times of earning and not earning, and between times
> of heavy family responsibilities and light or no family respon-
> sibilities.
>
> (HMSO 1942: para.449)

National Insurance would thus reaffirm the principle that
workers should pay for their own provision against poverty,
while the earmarking of contributions and their direct deduction
from the wage packet would make sure that 'the insured persons
should not feel that income for idleness, however caused, can
come from a bottomless purse' (ibid para.22).

Women and children last

The redistribution of resources within the working class was also
to be one of the principles by which the Beveridge Report was to
address some of the problems inherent within the wage system.
As Beveridge recognised, 'social insurance should be part of a
national minimum. But a national minimum for families of every
size cannot in practice be secured by a wage system, which must
be based on the product of a man's labour and not on the size of
his family' (ibid para.411).

The widespread existence of poverty and malnutrition, especially amongst families and children, which had been apparent

during the slump of the 1920s and 1930s had posed this problem sharply and indicated the state's difficulties in dealing with it. To make benefits when out of work adequate for subsistence, not only for individual workers but also for their dependants, was in the case of the low-paid and those with an above average number of children, to undermine the principle of less eligibility: to make relief more attractive than labour. The solution was to lie in a transfer of income from those without children to those with children, both in and out of work:

> The gap between income during earning and during interruption of earning should be as large as possible for every man. It cannot be kept large for men with large families, except either by making their benefit in unemployment and disability inadequate, or by giving allowances for children in time of earning and not earning alike.
>
> (ibid para.412)

The introduction of family allowances, later to be renamed Child Benefit – the subsidisation through the state of the families of both employed and unemployed workers – was thus to be the means of preserving the principle of less eligibility and of allowing a rise in the level of relief without confronting the wage system. In this sense the importance to the state of Child Benefit as a universal benefit, paid in respect of all children, has not been its adequacy in meeting the cost of bringing up a child, for as most studies have shown its value though diminished has never been sufficient, but in maintaining a differential between families with parents in and out of work. The declining value of Child Benefit from the late 1970s thus reflected governments' willingness to see the general level of subsistence lowered.

Nevertheless, the payment of family allowances breached an important principle which established the state's responsibility towards the financial maintenance of children, a development not unrelated to fears of a declining birth-rate (see Wilson 1977). In respect to other areas of domestic and family life, however, the Report although marking a new departure was far again from revolutionary.

In its treatment of women, the Beveridge Report was to enshrine within the system of post-war social security a systematic discrimination against women which, despite increasing and successful pressure for its removal, continues to inform the treatment of women. Behind this discrimination lay two major assumptions: that the proper role of women was as wives and mothers rather than workers, and that the economic status of women should be that of a dependence upon men.

In respect of his first assumption, Beveridge reflected a number of wider concerns that would inform other areas of social policy at the time (see Jones 1983). These included, on the one hand, a desire amongst policy-makers to remove women from their increasing war-time involvement in the paid labour market in order to minimise unemployment amongst men during peace-time, and, on the other, a fear of a declining birth-rate with its consequent longer-term shortage of labour. 'Taken as a whole', the Report therefore argued, 'the Plan for Social Security puts a premium on marriage ... The attitude of the housewife to gainful employment outside the home is not and should not be the same as that of the single woman. She has other duties ... In the next thirty years housewives as mothers have vital work to do in ensuring the adequate continuance of the British race and of British ideals in the world' (ibid para.114/7).

In support of this the Beveridge Report committed the state to the financial support of motherhood, with a maternity grant payable to all women, and maternity benefit for those who gave up paid work to have children. The treatment of married women other than in maternity, however, was one in which responsibility for their maintenance was assumed to lie with their husbands. Thus women, on marrying, were to lose any rights they previously had secured by way of contributions to the receipt of benefit. If they continued in paid work, they were allowed to be exempt from the National Insurance scheme – a clause which, until its abolition in the late 1970s established married women ironically as a particularly attractive and cheap form of labour. Where they continued to pay contributions, any subsequent benefit would be at a reduced rate, since they were not considered as independent householders, and where they were neither in work nor insured, their maintenance would be provided either through their husband's wage or through his benefit, which was increased to take account of her as a dependant.

Yet while the Beveridge proposals enshrined in legislation the

dependence of women – restricting and in important areas refusing them access to benefit, whilst paying benefit to the man
for them both – it was also significant at least in recognising the
importance of domestic work:

> In any measure of social policy in which regard is had to the
> facts, the great majority of married women must be regarded
> as occupied on work which is vital though unpaid, without
> which their husbands could not do their paid work and
> without which the nation could not continue.
>
> (ibid para.107)

'Vital though unpaid', the role of domestic labour in support of
paid work is crucial for the operation of capitalism. Its ideological
recognition in the Beveridge Report was significant, for it was
really the first government Report ever publicly to do so, and this
was to earn it the label of the 'Housewife's Charter'. But it was a
charter that did not give much in the way of financial recognition. Moreover, its assumption of the 'fact' that the 'great
majority' of married women were not involved in paid work,
while certainly not true of the war years, was to be even less so
over the following decades as the proportion of married women
in employment rose to over two-thirds. As we shall see later, the
continued discrimination against them within the social security
system has in part been responsible for making this experience
one of continuing poverty for women.

The limitations of the Beveridge Report, were ones of fundamental structure rather than just being incidental. To argue
therefore, as the system established after 1945 has been pro-
gressively eroded, for a 'return to Beveridge' as a solution to the
problem of poverty is to ignore these fundamental limitations. It
is also to ignore the fact that, despite the rhetoric, the Beveridge
Report and the Labour government's subsequent legislation was
never capable of eradicating poverty. While it would do something to extend the relief of poverty, it would leave the creation
of poverty unchallenged.

When the post-war Labour government, faced with pressure
from the United States' Marshall Plan to limit public expenditure, gave way to Treasury demands to reduce the rate of the
National Insurance Benefits below the poverty line and to limit
the duration for which they would be payable, two of the more

progressive aspects of the Beveridge Report were lost. The result was to be the creation in 1946 of an inadequate system of social insurance. When, moreover, in 1948 the Poor Law, which had been on the statute books for over three hundred years, was finally abolished in a fanfare of celebration, it turned out to be an abolition more in name than in principle. What Beveridge had argued would be a declining, and ultimately unnecessary role for special means-tested assistance as the insurance scheme spread, was to become an increasing large and important part of the social security system. In 1948 there had been one million claimants of means-tested assistance; by 1979 this had risen to three million and by 1987 to an estimated five and a half million, which including dependants made a total of over eight million people.

Social security and democracy

One of the most profound political developments over the last century and a half has been the growing demand for popular participation and control. From the Chartist and Suffragette movements, the achievement of the right to vote and to elect a government, through to demands for worker democracy and public participation, people have demanded the right to have a say in the institutions which affect their lives. The growth of social democracy was in part a reflection of this demand: it promised the extension of welfare as one of the rights of citizenship; it portrayed a state that would be accountable and responsive to people's needs; and it was consequently to be faced with mounting pressure to make its policies reflect the needs and interests of the majority.

The rise of the New Right in the 1970s was in large part to be predicted on a concern to limit the effect of democratic demands on the institutions of the state (see Sklar 1980; Jones 1983). Within the social democratic framework that until then had dominated many western governments in the post-war era, the problem of democracy had posed fundamental problems of control. The power of organised labour, the popular demand for more participation and involvement, and the democratic aspirations of members of organisations like the Labour Party forced an extension of democracy. At the same time, and especially in those particularly sensitive areas such as the relief of poverty, the attempt to shield the state from such pressures and to maintain a policy consistent with the requirements of capitalism involved constant manoeuvre and side-stepping.

Yet control of capitalism and the state has proved extremely elusive, and while social democracy has been an expression of the desire for control, it has in practice served to limit and contain it. It is not simply that the extension of democracy has given people only limited political rights such as the right to change their government every five years, whilst leaving the fundamental structures and inequalities of capitalism – and the power that goes with those – intact. Even within the state, control has remained beyond democratic reach. Faced with the majority pressure of democracy, and the conflicting need to maintain a social and economic system ultimately in the interest of a minority, the mechanisms of power and control have been forced deeper into the recesses of the state. Within the social democratic welfare state in general, the growth of professionalism and of rule by 'experts' has been a further mechanism whereby popular control has been frustrated. In the field of social security, perhaps more than most other areas of the welfare state, the need to shield its operation from democratic control has seen the increasing centralisation of its power and administration.

By the time that the Poor Law was formally abolished in 1948, most of its functions had already passed to other institutions. The 1920s and 1930s in particular had seen the politically sensitive issue of relief for the unemployed lead to the abolition of local democratic control through Boards of Guardians and the imposition of a new centralised authority. The issue had arisen as a result of the extension of the franchise beyond the propertied classes and the subsequent refusal of a number of Boards of Guardians predominantly in working class areas to follow central government guidelines to reduce levels of relief and to impose stricter conditions. During the early 1920s, with the serious prospect of unemployment amongst trained ex-service-men, and with a working class in defiant mood following the success of the Russian Revolution, the government had been uneager to act. With the defeat of the general strike in 1926, however, it moved quickly and introduced the Board of Guardians (Default) Act, making elected members personally liable for any unauthorised expenditure. The refusal to follow central government directives persisted, however, and in 1929 the 635 Boards of Guardians were abolished, to be replaced by 146 Public Assistance Committees of the local authorities, based on a geographically and socially wider electorate and with the power to co-opt experts and officials.

This move to limit local control of poor relief similarly failed to have the desired effect. When in 1931 the National Government imposed a 10 per cent cut in benefit levels for the unemployed and extended the Family Means Test, a number of Public Assistance Committees refused to toe the line, and in the words of the Minister of Labour 'are still persisting in a disregard of the law so complete that it would be impossible to condone it any longer' (cited Briggs and Deacon 1973:56). Accordingly, in 1934, in the face of considerable protest and opposition, especially from the National Unemployed Workers' Movement, relief for the unemployed was taken out of the hands of the Poor Law and placed in a central Unemployment Assistance Board (see Hannington 1978; Millett 1940).

The Board was to be an agency of the central state, with its own national administration, officials and finance, but although formally under the Ministry of Labour, it was not to be answerable for its administration to government, nor were the unemployed to have the right of independent appeal against its decisions. As Beveridge had argued before the 1932 Royal Commission on Unemployment Insurance:

> The relief of these men should be a matter, not of contractual right, enforced by quasi-legal process before an Umpire, but of need, judged by the administering authority, and would be subject to conditions imposed by the authority; the necessity of sidetracking detailed Parliamentary scrutiny of the actions taken in individual cases makes it desirable that this authority should be a commission with statutory power, and not a Minister directly responsible to Parliament.
>
> (Cited Millett 1940:30)

The 1934 Unemployment Assistance Board was thus to establish what the Poor Law Commission exactly a hundred years earlier had considered but felt unable to enact: a national and centralised system of relief for the unemployed. What was involved in this, however, was not a benign or impartial means of establishing national uniformity and administration, but a concentration of political power within the state in order to evade and attempt to defeat the political power of labour. In the first place the centralisation of relief was to remove not only local electoral control, but also seriously to weaken the ability of claimants to pressure directly for change in benefit levels and conditions. It was the local determination of relief which had been important in the successful organisation of the unemployed during the inter-war years, for it provided them with an identifiable focus for campaigns and activities (see Hannington 1936). The removal of local control was thus to have an important and limiting effect on the future organisation of claimants.

In the second place the setting-up of the Unemployment Assistance Board, like its successors in the National Assistance Board and the Supplementary Benefits Commission, involved the creation of an extra-parliamentary body with a considerable degree of autonomy. 'Though for obvious reasons no public pronouncement on the matter has been made in clear terms', revealed the Secretary to the Assistance Board in a confidential memorandum on the creation of the National Assistance Board in 1948, 'it is important that the administration of a service of this character should be insulated in some degree from gusts of generous but thoughtless sentiment, so that a humane but steady and rational policy can be pursued' (Reid 1948).

The decision 'to remove from direct political pressure' (ibid) the administration of means-tested assistance was maintained in 1966 when the Labour government refashioned the National Assistance Board into the Supplementary Benefits Commission. It was not to be the only example; in 1974 the *Sunday Times* reported on meetings held between 'over 100 civil servants, merchant bankers, chairmen of nationalised industries, politicians and academics' at which the problem had been posed of how to 'reconcile the short-term, essentially electoral preoccupations of democratically elected governments with the need for at least medium-term planning'. It went on:

There are those who simply want to take certain areas of planning and decision-making out of government itself and into government agencies that would be largely independent of parliamentary control – a process that has already gone some way in America. Over here, the creation of the Manpower Services Commission is a small step in that direction.

The elusiveness of power

The conflict between the demands of democracy on the one hand, and the requirements of capitalism on the other, has produced an increasingly centralised and bureaucratic system of social security (and of social welfare in general) that remains unresponsive to people's needs. This erosion of democratic control is a feature which successive post-war governments – Labour as well as Conservative – did little to challenge and much to reinforce. Yet it is also an issue which raises the question of the power and control exerted by elected governments themselves.

The state is of course much more than just a particular political party in government. As *The Times* in considering the record of successive Labour governments argued in 1977:

> The temptation for politicians taking office in peacetime to tinker with the government machine and to think, thereby, that they have effected a wider political transformation is very great and can be very damaging. It explains, for example, many of the illusions that accompanied Sir Harold Wilson's first ministry in 1964.
>
> (*The Times* 24th May 1977)

The government machine is never wholly within the control of elected politicians. This is something that even the avowedly right-wing Conservative administration under Margaret Thatcher at times found to its cost. Indeed the power and supposed interest of self-preservation of the civil service has for the New Right been a constant topic of debate and criticism, and has been identified as one of the major obstacles to radical change. For post-war Labour governments also the 'permanent politicians' of the senior civil service, as one of its former members has described them, the power of the judiciary, the police and the armed forces, as well as the weight and established traditions of bureaucracy, all exerted a powerful pressure to influence, delay, obstruct and even overturn democratic decisions.

At a more fundamental level than this, however, lies the power of capital and the requirements of the market. The Labour Party's commitment to the 'mixed economy' – even when, as it rarely did, it sought to go further than merely to provide a more efficient infrastructure for private capital – failed fundamentally to challenge this power, and as a result found itself constantly having to trim its policies to its demands.

At its most obvious level, this power is exercised directly through the power of wealth: in threatened 'runs on the pound' or in threats to withdraw investment or locate it elsewhere. It was not only in instances such as those where the Labour government, as *The Times* again put it, found itself 'on parole to the IMF' that this power was felt. The very existence of the market economy, with its principles of competition, of the private ownership of wealth and with its system of wage labour served to set 'constraints from which there is no escaping' (ibid). The state within such a framework inevitably found itself forced to balance the conflicting interests between labour and capital ultimately, although not without considerable difficulty, in the interests of the latter.

The state exists as a relatively autonomous institution – an autonomy that is exercised not only with respect to governments but also, as we have seen, with respect to particular interests and factions within the capitalist class itself, although it is an autonomy that is ultimately constrained within the parameters of capitalist production. In the final analysis, however, the state is less of an institution than a relationship of power: a relationship in which the exercise of control and decision-making has been taken away from the majority of the population, has been alienated from them, and stands as a power over them. The state is thus not the ultimate expression of democracy, but its negation. Its power incorporates the conflict between and domination of one group over another: of men over women, white over black, and capital over labour. In operating within and maintaining the existing structures, processes and relationships within society, the state invariably reproduces this domination and reinforces the position of those who benefit from it.

The failure of social democracy to appreciate the fundamental limitations involved in attempting to use the power of the state to change the structures of capitalism from within was to lead it to compromise and ultimately to the defeat of its purpose. The failure to effect 'an irreversible shift in the balance of wealth and power to working people', as the Labour Party's manifesto committed it, cannot be explained solely in terms of 'betrayals' or the timidity of leadership. Such a shift would have required the overturning of the basic structures and social relationships of the capitalist economy and of the state itself. It would have meant a mobilisation of working class power that, as the General Strike of 1926 or the Miners' Strike of 1984 showed, the Labour Party has forever been fearful of encouraging, and which Labour governments have at times done their most to suppress. The fact that successive Labour governments were unwilling to entertain such a prospect left them under mounting pressure to pursue more radical and progressive policies, but unable to go far enough and in such ways as to satisfy the demand. As a result it was to find itself facing increasing disillusionment and falling support.

Maintaining the incentive to work

The creation of the Supplementary Benefits Commission, like the National Assistance Board which it replaced, as a quango outside of day-to-day Parliamentary scrutiny, invested it also with considerable powers of its own. Within a very broad and general framework laid down in legislation, the Commission had the power to interpret this legislation, to issue its own regulations and to guide its officials in the conduct of their activity.

In some areas, as for example in the application of the cohabitation rule, departmental policy often preceded legislative sanction, with legislation being passed to legitimise existing practice. In other areas regulations are introduced without any further need for legislation. These regulations, the minutiae of social security policy and its administration have for most claimants always been the reality of social security. It is here, in the thousands of pit-falls and exclusions that fill page after page of social security manuals, in the intrusive questioning, and in the queues and stark surroundings of the social security office that the stigma of living on benefits is implanted and reinforced.

Since its origins, social security provision has held to an over-

riding concern to maintain the incentive to work. It has done so in
the face of the most extreme poverty and distress, and in the full
knowledge that, for many of those subjected to the wide variety
of pressures which it employs, work is simply not available.

In 1943 when discussion was taking place within the civil
service about the future post-war scheme of social security, one
senior civil servant argued that:

> there will be applicants for assistance whose need is wholly or
> partly due to their own actions – e.g. men who have left their
> last job voluntarily or have refused an offer of suitable
> employment... It would be wrong to base the whole
> administration of the scheme on the proper treatment of such
> cases. It will rather be for the Assistance Authority to evolve
> suitable techniques for hounding such delinquents.
>
> (Hutson 1943)

Over the following years, the evolution of such techniques has
reached impressive proportions. In the main, the pressures that
are used are reserved for the most vulnerable of the unemployed,
with increasing pressure being applied as claimants lose entitlement to unemployment benefit and become dependent on
means-tested Supplementary Benefit. The system of unemployment benefit, first introduced in 1911 to cater for the so-called
'genuine' and 'deserving' unemployed, has its own system of
controls and means of reinforcing the principle of less eligibility.
Apart from the low level of benefit itself and its payment for a
maximum of twelve months, the unemployed may have their
benefit suspended for a period of six weeks, extended since 1986
to thirteen weeks, where they are considered to be 'voluntarily
unemployed'.

Within the National Insurance scheme, the definition of
'voluntary unemployment' is laid down in law; it includes leaving
a previous occupation voluntarily, being sacked for 'industrial
misconduct' – 'a very strange sort of crime... Only a worker can
be accused of it, never an employer' (Kincaid 1973:222) – and
refusing an offer of 'suitable employment'. In 1985, 200,000
workers were to find themselves disqualified from benefit on
such grounds.

For those unemployed in receipt of means-tested Supplementary Benefit or Income Support – those without other house-

hold resources to fall back on, or who have exhausted or do not qualify for unemployment benefit – the situation is even less secure. Automatically, workers disqualified from unemployment benefit have any supplementary benefit for which they may be eligible reduced by 40 per cent. In addition, those considered to have refused an offer of 'suitable' work or training may have their benefit withdrawn altogether. On this clause alone some 220,000 claimants were refused Supplementary Benefit in 1985. Yet whereas the National Insurance scheme defines 'suitable' as work in a similar occupation and at an equivalent wage to that usually earned by a claimant, no such safeguard exists within the Supplementary sector. Benefit may be refused wherever officials may decide there is any sort of work available at any rate of pay. When pushed in the 1970s, amidst growing concern that such a rule was being applied in areas of high unemployment, to limit such action to cases where an actual job had been offered and refused, the Supplementary Benefits Commission replied:

> It was not possible to accept a recommendation about how the availability of suitable work should be tested since this would have largely obstructed the operation of the rule.
>
> (DHSS Annual Report 1973:70)

As the Supplementary Benefits Commission itself argued in evidence to the Parliamentary Committee on Abuse of Social Security Benefits, set up by Sir Keith Joseph in 1971 with the announcement that it would 'be after the layabouts and work-shirkers':

> There has to be a certain amount of pressure on claimants to find work and stay in it and it is a matter of hard fact that this involves letting it be known that state money is not there for the asking for anyone who is able to work but unwilling to do so while hotels, restaurants, cafes, shops and amusement centres are recruiting staff. The same thing applies in towns near farming areas where farmers need labourers for the harvest; wherever there are factories recruiting unskilled staff for labouring or packing or other simple work.
>
> (Report 1973:109)

The use of the benefit system to reinforce such low-paid work was a feature of social security provision throughout the post-war boom. Nor was it a practice confined to Conservative administrations: the introduction of the 'four-week rule' under a Labour government in 1968, limiting benefit for 'single fit unskilled men under the age of 45' to a maximum of four weeks, was just one example of a series of measures both continued and developed by Labour governments in the face of pressure from the media and other sources to crack down on supposed 'scroungers' and people abusing the system.

The complete withdrawal of benefit, such as applied to the single and the young, is less easily adopted as a pressure on those who have dependants to support. As the National Assistance Board noted in 1960:

> The most serious and intractable problem in the field of voluntary unemployment is that of the father of a large family who prefers a life of idleness. Not only does the size of the family mean that provision for its maintenance is a heavy burden on the community; the fact that a large number of children are growing up to regard idleness as a normal state of affairs cannot but cause concern. As the man's income while on assistance may often be not much less than it would be if he were to work ... he may have little financial incentive to find and keep a job ... If he is of an idle disposition, the extra few shillings which employment offers may not outweigh the disadvantages, as he sees it, of giving up a life of comparative freedom for the discipline of regular employment. Although drastic reduction, if not withdrawal, of the allowance might appear to be the obvious course, this is not acceptable if there are dependants who would suffer as a result. In the last resort, the only measure available to deal with the deliberate idleness of a man with dependants is the provision in section 51 of the National Assistance Act which makes it an offence for a person persistently to refuse or neglect 'to maintain himself or any person whom he is liable to maintain'.
>
> (Annual Report 1960:28)

Criminal prosecution of the unemployed under section 51, later section 30 of the Labour government's Supplementary Benefit Act, is not a very common affair – perhaps no more than twenty or thirty a year – but 'successful prosecutions, which are usually reported in local newspapers, also serve as a deterrent to others who might be tempted to follow the same course of idleness at the public expense' (Annual Report 1961:36). In addition, the receipt of the benefit for a claimant's dependants may be made conditional on attendance at a Re-establishment Centre - 'on the face of it', argued the National Assistance Board in 1953, 'an admirable instrument for dealing with the shirker as well as the weedy type of man'. As the Supplementary Benefits Commission acknowledged, such Centres are not intended to place people in work or to provide any vocational training: 'The sort of training they give is designed to revive the will to work, to restore the habit of getting up and going to work' (Annual Report 1975:74).

The application of these pressures is not confined to periods when plenty of work is available. Indeed, as unemployment began to rise in the 1970s, they were applied with even greater effort. Directed often against the most vulnerable of the un-employed, the fact that their cost-effectiveness in terms of benefit saved is far outweighed by the costs involved, is indication that such measures are not intended only, or perhaps even primarily, to deal with what is seen as the problem of a minority of claimants who are felt to be 'work-shy'. Rather they are measures designed to reinforce the stigma of less eligibility and to convey a message about dependence on the state as much to those who remain in employment as to those who are out of work. In the Report of the Committee on Abuse of Social Security Benefits, this issue was addressed directly with respect to the work of Unemployment Review Officers - special officials who work solely within the Supplementary Benefits scheme to review the cases of unemployed claimants:

> To what extent is it to the advantage of the community to spend public money in an endeavour to persuade or compel people to work who do not wish to work, at a time when there are many thousands who wish to work but cannot find work? ...
> The Unemployment Review Officer may be cost effective in the narrow sense of saving the cost of unemployment pay-ments to an individual, but has he reduced the cost of unemployment payments to society as a whole? If there are not enough jobs to go round, has he lowered the national level

of production by *pushing a reluctant, physically or mentally handi-capped, socially inadequate, or simply inexperienced man into a job* which might otherwise have gone to a man with the prospect of con-tributing more to production? . . . The problem has only to be stated in these terms to indicate how much is left out by the statement of it: the psychological damage to the individual of allowing him to recline [sic] on benefit and abandon the search for work; the general effect on public attitudes to work and self-help, and on the extent to which the whole notion of a social security system paid for out of taxes and/or contributions is called into question. We have had the advantage of discussions with officials of the DE and DHSS on this question, and they have told us of the views held by the regional controllers and those working under them, some in regions where unemploy-ment is especially high. They believe that society does benefit from the work of unemployment review officers and others in relation to the long-term unemployed, even in times and in areas of high unemployment.

(Report 1973:95. Emphasis added)

Divide and rule

The notion of a social security system that is divided between those benefits paid for by contributions and those paid, like Supplementary Benefit, from general taxation, is a notion that has long ceased to have any financial justification. Yet it is a distinction that is used in part to justify greater pressure and a much wider range of controls on those poorest of claimants who depend on means-tested assistance. With respect to the un-employed, these measures have been directed towards under-pinning the operation of the labour market, and in maintaining the unemployed as a reserve army of labour under constant pressure to take whatever jobs may be available. It is not, however, only in respect of unemployment that the social security system has operated to reinforce existing inequalities. Its promotion of certain forms of 'morality', its treatment of women and of black claimants, and its attitude in general to those dependent upon it have been powerful factors in dividing and fragmenting claimants and in shaping wider attitudes towards poverty.

Throughout the post-war period, successive governments were faced with increasing demand on the social security system. In part this was the result of demographic changes: a growing elderly population, changes in household composition such as an increasing number of single parent families, as well as continuing poverty and, from the early 1970s, rising unemployment. Some of these changes also reflected deeper social and cultural changes: changes in the role and expectations of women, in the attitudes of young people, in the erosion of the life-long nuclear family by increasing divorce or the desire of people to live alone or in other forms of household. Alongside these changes went a rising level of expectations, and an increasing confidence and ability to have those expectations satisfied. For most people, such expectations, for a greater degree of security, for an adequate and improving standard of living, were satisfied to a greater or lesser degree through the labour market. It was full employment, rather than the welfare state, which was the basis for increasing post-war living standards. For those outside the labour market, nevertheless, it was the welfare state that was to become a focus for demands and aspirations, and the state was thus forced to meet a growing pressure for more adequate levels of benefit and pensions, more responsive health and welfare services, and a more concerted attack on inequality.

Alongside this more directly political pressure, governments were to be faced with the problem of how to revitalise a sagging British economy and maintain economic growth. Here again the social security system – alongside other parts of the welfare state such as education or the health service – was to play an important role. The attempt by the Labour government under Harold Wilson in the mid 1960s to modernise British capitalism, and to use the power of the state to force it into 'the white heat of the technological revolution', while ultimately a failure, was to see, for example, the introduction of a new range of benefits – such as redundancy payments and earnings-related benefits – designed to protect in particular the more skilled and highly paid from the effects of the 'shake-out' of industry that was felt to be required.

Such measures reflected the kinds of pressure facing social democratic governments. On the one hand, the burden of economic restructuring was to fall upon labour, but on the other workers had, or at least had to be seen to be protected from its effects. That such legislation existed, no matter how inadequate or limited in its scope, was for many government supporters, so long as they did not probe too deeply, at least comforting evidence that something was being done to protect the vulnerable and the poor. What such provision also reflected was the particular support of social democracy within the Labour Party and trade union movement: a support which identified most readily with white, skilled male workers, and less readily with the unskilled, the unemployed, women and black workers.

The great proliferation of benefits that took place during the 1960s and 1970s, and the mounting piles of rules and regulations governing them, can be seen as an attempt both to meet and to contain these growing, and sometimes, conflicting demands. When faced with pressure, whether from the trade union movement, from public opinion, or from the growing range of pressure groups set up around the welfare state, the reaction of government was often to seek to limit the extent of change. Rather than respond to the demand for something to be done about poverty by increasing benefits in general, specific groups were singled out for attention, and a new range of benefits introduced. This not only increased the complexity of the system, and left those without powerful supporters at the bottom of an increasingly hierarchical system, it also allowed governments to respond to a demand for improvement by asking those who pressed for change, as did the Labour Secretary of State for Social Services, David Ennals, in 1977, to 'say which groups should be discriminated against to make way for their own priorities'.

The division and fragmentation of claimants is one way in which the social security system has attempted to divert and contain the growing demands placed upon it. Such divisions, of course, are not the creation of the social security system. From its origins the working class has been divided, but the maintenance and reinforcement of these divisions has been vital for the ability of capital to maintain its domination and to prevent a coherent and united challenge to its authority.

The division between men and women has been one of the most fundamental, by which both capital and the state, as indeed also men in general, have been able to take advantage of the unpaid labour of women in the home, and their weaker position as paid workers in the labour market. As we have seen, the foundations of post-war social security in the Beveridge Report embodied a dependent status for women, whose primary responsibilities were as wives and mothers, and whose involvement in paid work was either only temporary or as an additional contribution to the 'family wage'.

This role ascribed to women, although never a real reflection of women's lives, was to become even less so during the post-war decades. The entry of married women into the labour market, not for 'pin money' but often to maintain basic living standards, the growing number of single women, including those with children, and the growing consciousness of the women's movement with its demands for equality of treatment and the removal of discrimination, pressed hard against a state policy which continued to treat them as the dependants of men. This was, of course, true not only for married women, but also for single women and those who had become divorced or separated. In most such cases, state provision of benefit was to be offset by the search for 'liable relatives', most often ex-husbands, or male partners on whom the burden of support for children and for women without paid employment could be placed.

The Cohabitation Rule employed by the social security system was the inevitable corollary of its treatment of married women as dependent on their husbands. While its justification was that it would be unfair to deny benefits to married women, while allowing them to unmarried women living with men, the Cohabitation Rule was to go much further than simply to treat unmarried couples the same as married ones. Its power to deny benefit to single women suspected of cohabiting, and its obtrusive and personal questioning of women, as well as neighbours and others about their lifestyle and living arrangements, serve to convey, with considerable sanction, official messages about what kind of behaviour is accepted and tolerated.

In the case of the Cohabitation Rule, it has never been necessary for social security officials to demonstrate that a woman is actually being supported by a man before her benefit can be refused. As the DHSS has argued, 'the financial arrangement the couple come to in their relationship is not the point at issue'. Regardless of whether he is willing to support her, or she to be supported by him, 'it would be natural [sic] to expect that the man should, and in most cases would, accept the role of husband and support his "wife"'. It is moreover sufficient for a woman only to be suspected of cohabitation – according to the usual procedures by watching her house to see whether a man arrives at night or leaves in the morning, or by other evidence of his presence in the house – for her benefit to be denied or terminated; proof of cohabitation is not required. As the Committee on Abuse saw it, 'in a criminal prosecution guilt has to be proved beyond a reasonable doubt, whereas decision as to entitlements are taken on the balance of probabilities' (Report 1973:147), and in any case, 'if the claimant wishes to dispute the finding, she can appeal'. At the time, the period between termination of benefit and the hearing of an appeal was an average of three months.

The experience of black people within the social security system has equally been a history of intimidation and discrimination. Instructions such as that contained within the codes of guidance issued to officials to 'ask a claimant who *appears to have come from abroad* for the circumstances of his entry and any immigration conditions imposed. Examine his passport...' (emphasis added) inevitably focus on any claimant, whether foreign or British, who has not got a white skin. The additional impetus given by legislation such as the 1980 Nationality Act has served further to reinforce the role of the social security system as an extension of the immigration surveillance functions of the Home Office, and as a means whereby the British black population is scapegoated and its discrimination and division from the white working class yet further extended.

Racist practices are not confined to the social security system; yet their existence within a system which has such fundamental power over people's lives confirms the existence of racism as an institutional and structural feature of British society. According to a survey of Supplementary Benefit Offices by the Policy Studies Unit, the results of which were suppressed for a full year following protest from the DHSS, and only published after substantial editing especially of references to racism, 'Racist remarks were common from manager to doorman' (Cooper 1985:68).

The attitudes of social security officials towards women, black people and claimants in general are as important in conveying messages about the stigma of dependency as the bleak and forbidding atmosphere of social security offices or the structure and conditions of benefit. Not all of those who work for the DHSS are racist or sexist or punitive in their attitudes towards claimants; indeed the Civil Service unions within the DHSS have been at the forefront of campaigns during the 1980s to resist cutbacks in benefit and the tightening-up of relief. But the very structure of the social security system and its administration – the predominance of low-paid DHSS staff amongst those who deal directly with claimants, the pressures of increasing workload and declining staff numbers, the inevitable frustration and anger of claimants, and the system of rewards and promotion operated within the DHSS – all militate against a sympathetic approach to those in poverty. As one Higher Executive Officer put it:

> It's all right to talk about rights, but let me tell you that when you're faced with our sort of workload, all you're interested in is getting the job dealt with as best you can. It's all about numbers here, not rights.
>
> (Cited Cooper 1985:9)

Another official points to the pressure to take a hard line with claimants that is exerted through office managers:

> Last week he had me in; he'd been checking cases and come across one of my decisions. It was a woman who's had four Exceptional Needs Payments this year. He gave me a right dressing down because he said it was disgusting that she'd had four grants in the year and that it was obvious she was abusing the system ... He told me to watch all claimants for that in the future and to nil them [ie to refuse the claim] ... He reckons they'll soon get the message after one or two knockbacks. I don't agree with him. They're only like you and I, but I suppose I'll have to toe the line.
>
> (ibid:14)

The assumption that claimants are intent upon 'abusing' their position is endemic within the social security system, as also within the mass media. Many would argue that there are 'needy' and 'deserving' cases, but the very attempt to distinguish

between them and the disproportionate effort put into detecting
and controlling 'abuse' itself stigmatises and tars all claimants, to
such an extent that over a quarter of those with incomes below
the poverty line fail to claim even the minimum benefit to which
they are entitled.

As numerous studies have shown, the energy and commitment devoted by the social security system to the detection of
fraud and abuse is both grossly disproportionate to the amount
of fraud involved and far exceeds the effort expended by the state
to detect and prosecute the much more widespread fraud in areas
such as tax evasion. It is not just that the prosecution of fraud,
which, for example, doubled under the Labour government
between 1974 and 1979, is often accompanied by statements
such as that by Lord Justice Lawton to the effect that those found
guilty should 'expect to go to prison, even for a first offence . . .
[Social Security fraud] is rife from one end of the British Isles to
the other' (*The Times* February 1980). It is also that in its drives
against fraud and abuse the social security system has developed
a vast array of indiscriminate forms and procedures of investigation which, were they to be applied to those other than the
poorest and most vulnerable would be met with widespread
criticism and opposition. The random selection of claimants for
special investigation, the increasing number of fraud officers,
unemployment review officers, Specialist Claims Control units
and the like, and the singling out of particular groups such as the
homeless, the unemployed or single parents for greater scrutiny
reinforce the stigma of living on benefit and help sustain the
ideology of poverty as wilful idleness.

The impasse of social democracy

The aspirations of social democracy to create a more equal
society and its ultimate inability to do so were by the late 1970s to
set up a fundamental political impasse. Faced, on the one hand, by
pressures from the labour movement and by the growing
consciousnes, power and organisation of women, black workers
and the poor themselves, and, on the other by the demands and
requirements of a capitalist economy that was heading deeper
into crisis, the Labour government had no solution to offer. Each
step it took to accommodate its supporters was not large enough,

and only intensified frustrations and the demand for more decisive action. Each step it took to satisfy the demands of capital further undermined its support and lead to increasing disillusionment and scepticism.

In many ways, the failure of social democracy was inevitable. It was a form of politics which first and foremost failed to recognise the inherent conflicts and inequalities of a capitalist society. As Miliband and Liebman (1985/6) describe it:

> For most social democratic politicians, capitalist society (in so far as the existence of capitalism is acknowledged at all) is not a battlefield on which opposed classes are engaged in a permanent conflict, now more acute, now less, and in which they are firmly on one side, but a community, no doubt quarrelsome, but a community nonetheless, in which varied groups – be they employers, workers, public employees – make selfish and damaging demands, which it is the task of government to resist for the good of all.

This failure to recognise the fundamental and irreconcilable divisions within capitalism does not mean that the problems thrown up by these divisions and conflicts disappear. Moreover, the failure to recognise their origins has often meant that in seeking solutions to such problems, social democratic governments have done so at the expense of the weakest and the politically least threatening of the protagonists.

Thus in its analysis of poverty, social democracy does not recognise an irreconcilable clash of interests; nor does it see poverty as an intrinsic and essential part of the way in which the economy operates. Rather, poverty is seen as a mal-distribution of resources, to be corrected by state intervention and provision. In dealing with poverty only as a consequence of capitalist relations, and not as a precondition for capitalism, its attempts to deal with the problem of poverty were inevitably limited. Moreover, its attempts to do something about the problem remained within the confines of capitalist social relations. As a result, post-war social democratic governments were frequently to be found rationing resources between competing groups of the 'quarrelsome community', allowing one group to be played off against another, and allowing its intervention to be limited by the parameters of the labour market and the ideologies supporting it.

What success social democracy achieved was dependent on growth. So long as the economy was expanding, then it was possible to improve conditions and extend benefits for the poor without seriously challenging the structures and distribution of inequality and wealth. So long as the cake kept growing, the poor would get a bigger piece than before, even though their share of the cake would remain the same. Given the sheer scale of inequality, the redistribution of income and wealth through taxation and welfare even during the boom years of the post-war period resulted in remarkably little change. What change there was, moreover, tended to be from the very rich to the rich and better-off. The relative position of the poorest, both in and out of work, remained more or less constant. When the boom came to an end, their position was to deteriorate even further. During the four years of Labour government between 1976 and 1979, for example, the poorest twenty per cent of the population were to see their share of 'original' income fall from 0.8 per cent to 0.5 per cent, while even their share of 'final' income, after taxation and welfare provision are both taken into account, fell from 7.4 per cent to 6.9 per cent. Over the same period, the share of marketable wealth owned by the bottom fifty per cent of the population remained constant at 5 per cent (*Social Trends* 1985).

The thirty years of the welfare state after 1945 did little to alter the fundamental inequalities of capitalism. Perhaps what it did do was at least to prevent the poor from falling significantly farther behind. It also, or at least for certain important groups, helped to alleviate some of the insecurity of wage labour and removed some of the stigma of the Poor Law. In areas such as the National Health Service or in education, it provided coverage and opportunities for many who, either previously or under a free market system, would otherwise have been excluded, and it introduced certain principles – principles of free access, of mutual responsibility, of 'rights' and of the value and dignity of human beings – which, however incomplete in their conception and inadequate in their implementation, nevertheless represented significant gains.

But these gains were also all made at significant cost. As the cost of providing welfare was shifted not just further onto the shoulders of the working class, but within the working class onto the shoulders of the poor and low-paid, so divisions and tensions between those receiving benefits and those paying for them – often not very different in their standards of living – were reinforced. The cost has to be counted too in the way in which state welfare, while it increased security for some, was able to maintain the pressures of insecurity and poverty for others, and thus buttress the operation of an unequal labour market or the sexual and racial divisions of labour. For those dependent on the welfare state the cost of dependency was also to be the loss of autonomy and control: it meant to be at the whim of officials, subject to personal investigation and moral scrutiny, and dependent on the slow movements of a vast bureaucracy which, while it claimed to have people's welfare at heart, seemed often to treat them with indifference or contempt.

When the Conservative Party under the new leadership of Margaret Thatcher entered the 1979 election campaign with the slogan 'Get the state off our backs', it found considerable support, not least amongst those on whose backs the state sat most heavily. That many of the poor or many of the working class in general did not see the welfare state as 'their' welfare state to defend – that campaigns and demonstrations fizzled out without mass support – should not have caused any great surprise. That the Conservative Party, and the right wing in general, were able to identify the welfare state with 'socialism' made it even harder for the Labour Party to fight back. The welfare state never was socialism; the idea that it could exist as an island of socialism in a sea of capitalism proved as false as the idea that capitalism could simply be legislated out of existence.

THATCHERISM AND THE NEW CAPITALISM

The attack on expectations; economic restructuring and social security; benefits as a political weapon; rights or discretion?; the 1986 Social Security Act; a continuing programme; the two-thirds society.

There is far too much talk about rights, whether they be welfare rights or the rights to withdraw one's labour.
(Peggy Fenner, M.P., in the debate on the Social Security Act, House of Commons, April 1980)

The election of the Conservative government in 1979 marked a turning-point in the history of social security and of the welfare state in general: a turning-point as significant as that of the 1830s, of the Liberal reforms immediately before the First World War, and of the Labour government immediately after the Second World War. Like these previous periods, it was to attempt a major restructuring of the welfare system, and like them also this was to take place in the context of major economic, social and political change.

It has often been said that history repeats itself: the first time as tragedy, the second time as farce. Yet while there is much in the 'Thatcher revolution' to recall earlier themes of less eligibility, 'Victorian values' and a demand for a reduced role of the state, there is little that is farcical about its impact and intentions. The government that came to power in 1979 was committed to a reversal of what were themselves only limited post-war trends towards greater equality, to a dismantling of the protective elements of state welfare, to breaking the power of the organised labour movement and to a reaffirmation of the primacy of market forces that would bring poverty and unemployment to unprecedented levels.

It is equally true that while history may repeat itself, it does not do so under the same conditions. While the intention of the New Right was to break the impasse of social democracy and shift the balance of power back in favour of capital, its attempt to do so was to take place in a very different context – for both capital and labour – than that of previous periods of social reform.

Since at least the mid-1960s onwards capitalism, both in Britain and in the rest of the world, has been involved in a major process of restructuring. Partly as a response to the conditions and problems created for it by the post-war boom, picking up speed with the onset of economic slump in the 1970s, and accelerating at an even greater pace during the 1980s, this restructuring has initiated fundamental and long-term changes in the operation of the economy and the structure of the labour market.

These changes have involved not only a regional and a national but also an international dimension, with capital's ability to shift investment and capacity around the globe giving it a powerful weapon to dictate terms and conditions. At the same time, the structure of employment has been markedly changed, with the post-war patterns of permanent full-time employment for a large majority being replaced by the creation of a large permanent pool of unemployed and an increasing reliance on casual, part-time and temporary labour. Thus during the 1970s, for example, the British economy shed 800,000 full-time jobs, while the number of part-time jobs increased by over one million. Contained within this was also a shift in the composition of the workforce, for, unlike the jobs which were lost, the new jobs were overwhelmingly low-paid jobs carried out by women. By reducing their permanent workforces to a core of primary and usually skilled male workers, and by sub-contracting out the supply of components or services to other, smaller businesses as well as through the increasing use of temporary, casual and part-time labour, employers have sought to cope with the fluctuations and instability in markets and to overcome the obstacles of protective legislation and workers' organisation.

The Conservative government that was elected in 1979 faced an economy that was already rapidly restructuring itself in the face of economic crisis and working class power. It also confronted a welfare state and a balance of political power that had been unable to reconcile the conflicting demands of capital and labour. The impasse of social democracy – the inability of the previous Labour government either to confront effectively the direction in which capital was taking it or to defeat the strength and aspirations of labour which this direction required – provided the New Right with its opportunity.

The attack on expectations

The fundamental assault on the expectations and achievements of working people that characterised the policies of the Conservative government from 1979 onwards is not unique to Britain. In West Germany, the United States and elsewhere, the resurgence of a new, aggressive right-wing politics has seen the attempt to resolve the crisis of capitalism through confrontation with organised labour, through a re-assertion of racism and a reimposition of the domestic ideology of women, and through attempts to break the power of trade unions and to shift the balance of class forces firmly in favour of employers. It has also involved the attempt to redefine the responsibilities of the state: to get rid of the notion, however imperfectly it was realised in practice, that the state had a legitimate role and responsibility in ensuring greater equality and fairness or in protecting workers from the consequences of an unbridled capitalism. Perhaps above all, it has involved an assault on popular expectations that built up with increasing rapidity during the boom that followed the Second World War: on expectations of security and employment, of rights to protection and welfare provision, and of meaningful progress towards equality of race and gender.

In 1975 the Trilateral Commission – a select international body of leading politicians, civil servants, industrialists and social scientists – added weight to a growing belief amongst the international ruling class that the problems facing the industrialised west stemmed from a growth in expectations that neither capitalism nor the social democratic state could contain. In its report entitled *The Crisis of Democracy* it attempted to explain the apparent paradox between increasing material progress and rising social tensions and conflict:

> Three main factors seem necessary to account for the paradox. First, as happens everywhere, change produces rising expectations which cannot be met by its necessary limited outcomes. Once people know that things can change, they cannot accept easily anymore the basic features of their condition that were once taken for granted. Europe has been especially vulnerable, since its unprecedented economic boom had succeeded a long period of stagnation with pent-up feelings of frustration. Moreover, its citizens have been more sophisticated politically...
>
> (Cited Jones 1983b:5)

This sophistication, moreover, had placed increasing demands on the state to take more and more decisions, yet 'decisions do not only bring power; they also bring vulnerability. The modern European state's weakness is its vulnerability to blackmailing tactics' (ibid).

As we have already seen, one response to this was to seek to remove areas of decision-making from the political arena. But the expectations that post-war capitalism and the welfare state had helped generate, although not resolved, were to remain. They were also, within this right-wing analysis, to create not just a crisis of unresolved expectations, but also a fundamental crisis of culture.

Lord Young, previously appointed by Margaret Thatcher to chair the Manpower Services Commission, before he was elevated to the House of Lords to become the government's spokesperson on employment issues, put his finger on one aspect of this when he said, 'I believe very strongly it's because of our culture, because of the sort of circumstances in the '50s, particularly the '60s and '70s, when profit-making, making money, was not quite nice.' The popular revolt against capitalism and its values – berated throughout the early 1980s by leading figures of the Conservative Party as the product of the 'permissive society' – was, however, much more widespread than just a questioning of its economic priorities. It also encompassed a fundamental questioning, and rejection, by women of their allotted inferior position in a male-dominated world; it saw young people demanding acknowledgement and a relationship with adults (whether as parents, teachers or employers) based on negotiation rather than unquestioned authority; it witnessed the rise of civil rights movements, and the demands of black, gay and other people to be treated equally, fairly and with respect. This blossoming of a popular political culture, fundamentally threatening as it was to many established and vested interests, was to be identified as the cause of economic and social ill.

Just as the political economists of the early nineteenth century had recognised that capitalism was not just an economic system, but also a system of social and political relationships bound together by certain forms of morality – by ideas and attitudes and behaviour – so the rise to power of radical right-wing governments in the late 1970s and early 1980s was to place the dismantling of expectations and the creation of a new 'morality' high on the agenda. Significantly, one of the first acts of the new British government in 1979, alongside its promise to curb the trade unions and to increase the 'flexibility' of the labour market, was to introduce legislation dealing with social security.

Economic restructuring and social security

Although registered unemployment in Britain already stood at a post-war record level of over one million when the Conservative government took office in 1979, over the short space of the next two years it was to double. While external economic factors played some part in this, by far the greatest cause of this acceleration was a deliberate government-induced recession, brought on by a restrictive monetary policy, that was to produce a virtual collapse in manufacturing industry. Wave after wave of redundancies and lay-offs, together with political restrictions on the activities of trades unions were to deal a severe blow to the strength and confidence of workers and their ability to resist.

The 1980 Social Security Acts introduced by the new Conservative administration were to be a part of this process. Through legislation, administrative change, propaganda and ideology it was to attempt to refashion the social security system, and in particular those parts of it that dealt with the unemployed, the young, women and the poorest, in accordance with the new requirements of capital and its changing political economy.

The 1980 Acts, of which there were two, were, among
things, to break the link between benefits and rising
standards, by uprating benefits only in line with prices r
than wages. They also cut the level of unemployment and o
short-term benefits by 5 per cent and abolished the payment
earnings-related supplements to benefit. This cut in benefit (the
first since the 10 per cent cut in benefit imposed by the National
government in 1934) was justified by the Minister of State, Patrick
Jenkin, on the grounds that benefits should be taxable, and that
the cut was 'in lieu of taxation', despite the fact that many of those
in receipt of benefit would not have found themselves liable to tax.
When the taxation of benefits was formally introduced, however,
the cut was, predictably, not restored.

The abolition of earnings-related supplements to unemployment, sickness, widows' and maternity benefits, despite the con-
tinuation and even a 1 per cent increase in earnings-related contributions, was even further to undermine the notion of National
Insurance benefits as guaranteed by contributions. As far as the
unemployed were concerned, the earnings-related supplement –
introduced by a Labour government in 1966 in order to ease the
impact of redundancy on the more highly skilled and more highly
paid workers – had by 1979 ceased to be either as widespread or
as significant in amount. In 1971, for example, this supplement
had succeeded in raising unemployment benefit for those who
qualified for it from 45 per cent to 70 per cent of net average earnings, by 1980 the figures were only 33 per cent and 46 per cent
respectively.

The declining value of and numbers of unemployed eligible for
earnings-related supplement itself reflected the changing composition of the unemployed. Unemployment is not random; it is
concentrated most heavily on the low-paid and the unskilled, and
it is on these groups – and especially on women, black workers
and the young – that the burden has fallen disproportionately as
unemployment has risen. Manual workers, for example, are six
times more likely to be unemployed than non-manual workers,
even within the same occupation black workers are twice as likely
to be refused a job as their white counterparts, while the average
earnings of those out of work, assuming they could find a job, is
only two-thirds of the national average.

At the same time, increasing unemployment has also meant an

...n of unemployment. In 1965 16 per cent of the
...yed had been out of work for a year or more; by
18... 300,000, and by 1987 more than a third of over
...ut of work were to be counted amongst the long-
...loyed. The time limit on unemployment benefit,
...her with the exclusion from benefit of those such as
...nen without sufficient full-time and continuous em-
..., has meant an increasing reliance of the unemployed
...eral means-tested benefit. By 1986 only one-quarter of
...unemployed were receiving any unemployment benefit: the
remainder having to turn to Supplementary Benefit for support:
proportions that were almost exactly reversed during the 1960s.
When in 1980 the government bowed to mounting pressure to
extend the long-term rate of supplementary benefit to those
claimants dependent on benefit for over a year, rather than two
years as previously, long-term unemployed claimants continued
to be excluded: a discrimination that persisted in the second
major revision of benefits in 1986.

This treatment of unemployed claimants in particular both
reflects and reinforces wider trends in the structure of the labour
market. From the 1970s onwards it began to appear that,
contrary to much of both left and right-wing orthodoxy, rising
unemployment had little effect in reducing wage levels. After an
initial check in the early 1980s, average real wage settlements
continued to rise, despite unprecedented levels of unemployment. Yet this co-existence of high unemployment and increasing average wages masked an increasingly polarised labour
force and the differential effect of unemployment on those in
work. This trend within the labour market, indicated earlier,
increased even more rapidly during the first half of the 1980s:
between 1981 and 1985 a further one million full-time permanent jobs were lost, while the proportion of those employed on a
temporary, part-time or casual basis increased to 34 per cent of
the workforce. By 1985 one-quarter of all men and one half of all
women in work did not have permanent full-time employment.

The pressure of unemployment (at least in terms of wages,
since the threat of the sack was to be used throughout industry
to bring about changes in working practices and conditions, not
least of which was the imposition of a more polarised workforce)
was thus to be felt differentially amongst those in work. Between

1979 and 1984, for example, the earnings of non-manual workers rose by 85 per cent – more than 20 per cent above the rate of inflation – while the earnings of manual workers barely kept pace with price rises, and for certain groups showed an actual decline. In real terms the average earnings of the highest-paid ten per cent of workers increased by 22 per cent between 1979 and 1986, those of the lowest-paid ten per cent by 3 per cent. In 1983 three million full-time workers were in low-paid work: two-thirds of them women; if the full-time equivalent wage of part-time workers was to be included, the figure would have risen to six million.

The growing polarisation between a primary or core group of more highly paid and predominantly male workers, shielded to a greater extent from market forces and the pressures of unemployment by internal recruitment and promotion systems, and a secondary or peripheral labour market of deskilled, low-paid, part-time and casual work thus created the conditions for an increasing assault on the security and living standards of the unemployed. The concentration of unemployment, and its effects, on the secondary labour market, the political powerlessness of the unemployed and their relative isolation from the organised labour and trade union movement (largely organised within the primary labour market), enabled increasing financial and other pressures to be applied against them by the social security system. Few powerful voices were raised in protest as, from 1979 onwards, the new government increased the range and number of so-called fraud investigators and whipped up a media campaign of hysteria about social security scrounging and abuse.

The Conservative government's strategy was both to accept and assist capital's restructuring. Implicit within this was an acceptance of low-paid and insecure employment reinforced by the pressures of unemployment for a large, and growing, proportion of the population. The acceptance of that meant a reduction in the range and level of benefits for those unemployed. As the Prime Minister Margaret Thatcher revealed in 1980, 'I believe it was right to cut the increase in unemployment benefit, because I believe that it is right to have a larger difference between those in work and those out of work'. Within its first two years of office, according to an analysis presented in *The Times* in 1981, the total value of state support for an unemployed couple with two children had fallen by 40 per cent.

Benefits as a political weapon

The use of benefits as a means of reinforcing a low-paid labour market or of constructing attitudes towards women or poverty is itself highly political, although this may often be disguised under talk of the 'needs of the economy', of the 'natural' role ascribed to certain groups, or of fecklessness and scrounging. With the 1980 Social Security Acts, however, the new Conservative government was to bring the benefit system into much more overt means of political manipulation. In particular, it was to introduce new regulations covering the payment of benefit to workers on strike as part of its policy to break the power of organised labour.

The payment of benefit to strikers has, since the days of the Poor Law, been both highly circumscribed and limited in its extent. Under all governments in Britain strikers themselves have never been allowed to claim weekly benefit: at most, benefits have been paid to dependants, and single one-off payments to strikers themselves only in cases of urgent necessity. Even then, few workers on strike look to the social security system for support. In most cases, strikes are relatively short, and it is on previous earnings, savings, the wages of wives or husbands and borrowing from family or friends that most look to see them through a dispute. In a study of all strikes between 1950 and 1972 which lasted for more than two weeks (themselves a minority of disputes) it was shown that less than a quarter of those on strike with dependants to support had income sufficiently low to qualify for benefit, and even then only about one in ten of those who qualified actually claimed benefit (Gennard and Lasko 1974:11). Even the traditionally militant Engineering Employers Federation admitted that 'even where a Union encourages its members to apply for state support, it is clear that Supplementary Benefit provides only a minority – perhaps seldom more than a quarter – of the average income of a striker's family'.

Clause 6 of the 1980 Social Security Act, however, sought to reduce even further the benefits that those on strike could claim. As the Minister of State Patrick Jenkin argued in introducing the legislation, this clause was 'in a totally different category from the remainder of the Bill', for whereas its other clauses were justified in terms of reducing public expenditure,

Clause 6 'will save public money to a modest extent, but that is not its main concern. The government was elected, amongst other things, to restore a fairer bargaining balance between employers and trade unions. Clause 6 represents one of the steps taken to that end' (*Hansard* 15th April 1980).

Accordingly, the 1980 Social Security Act abolished the right of those on strike, or locked out of work by their employers, to claim an urgent needs payment and introduced a compulsory £12 deduction, to rise each year with inflation, in any benefit payable to the dependants of any worker involved in, or even standing to benefit from, an industrial dispute. 'If it is suggested', argued Patrick Jenkin, 'that in certain circumstances the individual or union cannot afford it, the answer is simple. There is the choice not to strike, to go back to work and earn the living that is available'.

The introduction of Clause 6 was one significant example of the way in which the new Conservative government's legislation formed part of an overall and considered strategy of confrontation with organised labour that had been in preparation since the early 1970s. The reasons behind its action had been spelled out in a series of reports and discussion papers circulating within the Conservative Party during its years of opposition between 1974 and 1979. These pointed to a growing belief on the right that the strength of organised labour, especially within the state-owned nationalised industries, was the greatest obstacle to a restructuring of the British economy and a dismantling of the protective elements of state welfare. In particular they were a response to what had been seen as the humiliating defeat of the Conservative government under Edward Heath by the miners' strikes of 1972 and 1974. In the final report of a Conservative Party policy group chaired by Nicholas Ridley, and leaked to *The Economist* in May 1978, for example, it was argued that confrontation with workers in the nationalised industries was inevitable, and that 'the most likely battleground will be the coal industry... The greatest deterrent to any strike', it continued, 'would be to cut off the money supply to the strikers'.

Of all groups of workers, the miners have occupied a special place in the history of the organised labour movement in Britain in the twentieth century. They have been seen both as a vanguard of labour's struggle for better pay, security and safer working conditions and as representative of the gains that have been made. Significantly the National Union of Mineworkers has also been the union which has made most claim for the right of its members on strike to claim relief from the state. During the 1970s, for example, payments to strikers' dependants averaged £2 million a year; yet in 1972 and 1974, both years of major disputes in the mining industry, such payments rose to £8 million and £5 million respectively. Similarly the granting of urgent needs payments to strikers without dependants numbered 52,000 in 1972, as opposed to 5,000 for the whole of the previous ten years.

The preparation and planning of the Conservative strategy to break the power of organised labour, of which Clause 6 was but one amongst many parts, came to fruition in 1984 in one of the most bitter and prolonged disputes of the twentieth century. With the threat of mass unemployment established as a weapon to intimidate working class militancy, a series of legislation limiting the power of trade unions and outlawing supportive action, and the changes introduced by the 1980 Social Security Acts firmly on the statute books, the whole weight of the state – from riot police to welfare offices – was thrown against the year-long miners' strike (see Jones and Novak 1985). The defeat of the miners, whilst not wholly decisive and unambiguous, marked a significant step in the Conservative counter-revolution.

Rights or discretion?

'The translation of a want or need into a right', has argued the right-wing politician Enoch Powell, 'is the most widespread and dangerous of modern heresies' (Powell 1972:11). Whether it is 'modern' depends on the time-scale adopted, for certainly since the origins of capitalism, through the riots of the 1820s and 1830s, the attempt to secure a Right to Work Bill in 1908, the 'Right to Work or Full Maintenance' campaign of the NUWM during the inter-war years, and the welfare rights movement of the post-war period, a working class dependent on wage labour has demanded either the right to work or, failing that, the right to be provided with an adequate standard of living.

Although they seek to create a greater dependence upon it,

even those on the right acknowledge that the market system of capitalism cannot meet everyone's needs. To the extent that capitalism distributes resources according either to paid labour or the ownership of wealth, those without wealth and unable for whatever reason to engage in wage labour are left with their needs unmet. While the state throughout history has always sought to place the responsibility for meeting such needs as far as possible onto others, and in particular onto the family, it has nevertheless been compelled to make at least a minimal level of provision itself. One of the central problems for the state, however, has been how to prevent the satisfaction of such needs being turned from a matter of discretion into a matter of right. For, as Powell argued, to turn a need for work or income into a right to work or income is for capitalism extremely dangerous; it is to undermine the insecurity and methods of discipline on which the labour market depends, and to remove from the state its power to condone or condemn certain forms of morality and behaviour. Just as when workers have the right to a job, the disciplinary power of employers is greatly reduced, so once people have the right to receive benefit, the discretionary power to offer or refuse it according to character, prejudice, morality or some other test of dessert is lost.

The translation of wants or needs into rights, while not new, is a struggle that has achieved increasing success. Its victories have only ever been partial, and the decision of the state to accede a right to any particular group has often been taken only to avoid an otherwise irresistible pressure that threatened to secure it for the rest. In 1911 the 'right' to benefit (although as we have seen, still with considerable qualification and conditions) was extended to most male workers in respect of sickness and a minority of male workers in respect of unemployment benefits. In the 1920s and again in 1946 these 'rights' were further extended, although again only on condition that sufficient contributions had been paid, and subject to a number of limitations that severely circumscribed their adoption as a universal right to income from the state for those unable to earn a living.

In all these developments the gains that were made were more to the benefit of the more organised and more powerful sections of the working class. When the post-war welfare state extended the notion of a right to education or a right to health care, these again were to benefit disproportionately the politically powerful and more highly paid, especially amongst the expanding white collar and middle classes.

For the poorest, the right to relief was to remain much more elusive. In 1964 Labour's successful election manifesto pledged an Income Guarantee 'as of right... in the first few weeks of a Labour government' (cited Kincaid 1973:64). A year and a half later, the discretionary relief provided by the National Assistance Board was replaced by a Supplementary Benefits Commission. Although the 1966 Social Security Act which set up the Commission talked of 'entitlement' to benefit, this was still to be conditional on a means test, and even when, and if, that was satisfied, the right to a supplementary benefit was extended only to old age pensioners. For whereas once the elderly had demonstrated their need a supplementary pension had to be paid, in the case of all other claimants the Commission was given the wide and general power to reduce or withhold benefit in 'exceptional circumstances': the interpretation of which was left largely to its discretion.

This power of discretion has, as we saw in the last chapter, not only been used to deny claimants a right to benefit. It has also, in its power to increase payments to particular individuals in need, been an important mechanism for maintaining a low basic rate of benefit for the remainder. The ability of the Supplementary Benefits Commission to grant both additions to the weekly rate of benefit (for example for heating or special dietary needs) and one-off payments (for clothing or furniture), meant that successive governments were able to keep the basic rate of benefit down to the minimum for day-to-day survival.

By the end of the 1970s, however, the declining value of the basic benefit in relation to general living standards, together with the increasing organisation and confidence of claimants in their demands for welfare 'rights', was to put increasing pressure on the system and lead to an escalating level of discretionary payments. In 1968 weekly additions to benefit were being paid to 540,000 claimants; by 1979, even though the total number of claimants increased by only 100,000, the number receiving weekly additions had risen to 2,252,000; over the same period the cost of one-off single payments had risen from £2 million to £38 million. Although the latter represented less than half of one per cent of the social security budget, its symbolic importance, and the fact that it was a payment made primarily to the unemployed and to single mothers – the most undeserving of the undeserving poor – meant that the cost involved became a minor issue. What had previously been seen as 'exceptional' payments at the discretion of the SBC had in practice become the norm for nearly half of all claimants, while the refusal of such payments had, in the words of a review commissioned by the Labour government in 1978, 'become one of the main causes of friction between claimants and staff' (Social Assistance 1978:13).

One of the features of Conservative policy after 1979 which did much to disable opposition was its ability to claim that many of its measures simply reflected what the previous Labour government had either proposed or attempted. This was no less true for social security, and in 1980 the Conservative government applied the general conclusions of the Social Assistance Report to its legislation. The Supplementary Benefit scheme, which ever since Beveridge had formally been portrayed as a residual part of the social security system, was now to be adapted to its 'mass role' in dealing with poverty. Crucial in this was to end the ability of claimants to exert pressure on local officials to make discretionary payments in addition to the basic benefit. As the Minister Lynda Chalker made clear:

> I want to make sure that the outcome of a request for an Exceptional Needs Payment does not depend on the persuasiveness of the claimant or his advocates ... The regulations must be made absolutely clear
>
> (Cited *Social Work Today* 30/7/1984)

Accordingly, the discretionary power of officials was substantially curtailed, and replaced instead by a series of Regulations which in painstaking and impenetrable detail sought to lay down the considerably restricted conditions under which a particular claimant might qualify for a particular payment. The result was not only to be chaos and irregularity, as Benefit Officers struggled to understand and cope with the mass of Regulations (or simply ignored them), but in the short-term a substantial loss to claimants. Certain aspects of benefit were particularly hard-hit: the payment of clothing grants, for example, fell from 360,000 in 1979 to a level three years later (during which time the number of claimants had almost doubled) of less than a fifth of that amount.

It is a feature of many areas of social policy that decisions taken by governments do not always have the desired effect. While the shift from discretionary payments to regulations had an immediate result in depressing claims for benefit, it also appeared to establish quite quickly a right to such payments that was clearly laid down for those who qualified. In 1981, the year after the new Regulations were introduced, less than a quarter of claimants had successfully claimed a single payment; by 1984, however, the number had risen back to over a half, including three-quarters of non-pensioner households. Weekly additions had similarly risen to be paid to 60 per cent of all claimants by 1983 (HMSO 1985 Vol II:18). By 1985 recognition of the failure of tightly-controlled regulations to halt the rise in additional payments was to put them once again under scrutiny. According to the major review then initiated by the Secretary of State Norman Fowler:

> The rapid growth in payments over the last few years has raised considerable questions of fairness with those not on benefit. The availability of payments for those on benefit stands in sharp contrast to the position faced by many others, on what may not be very different levels of disposable income
>
> (Ibid:22)

In the context of an increasing number of low-paid workers, who remained ineligible for such payments, this 'unfairness' was to be resolved by scrapping the regulations and removing the right to such payments for those on benefit.

The 1986 Social Security Act

Despite its claim to be the most thorough-going review of the social security system since the Beveridge Report, the review of social security undertaken under the auspices of the Secretary of State Norman Fowler in 1985 was silent on a number of major areas of policy. Despite a long-standing recognition that there are two mechanisms through which the state redistributes income – the system of taxation and tax reliefs on the one hand, and the social security system on the other – the review was to concentrate only on the latter. Even within this, the review and its subsequent legislation was to take a particular focus. Apart from its thwarted proposals to abolish SERPS – the State Earnings Related Pension Scheme – the universal basic state pension was left untouched, although it accounted for half of total social security expenditure. Similarly, the main National Insurance benefits for sickness and unemployment received little attention. Certainly the National Insurance benefits, like the basic state pension, had, since the 1980 Social Security Acts broke the link with average earnings, failed to keep pace with living standards and were destined to continue to fall in value. Nevertheless, the unwillingness of the government directly to confront such universal benefits, despite the large part they play in the social security system and the fact that they consume the majority of its expenditure, and to concentrate instead on benefits for the poorest, was an indication not only of its priorities but also of its political vulnerabilities.

In its review of means-tested benefits, the Fowler Report was to seek to consolidate means-testing as a way of dealing with the problem of mass poverty and to limit its areas of growth. Supplementary Benefit was to be renamed Income Support, and the Report was to propose a series of changes that would lead to a more rigid and tightly controlled system of relief.

Many of those who gave evidence to the review stressed the complexity, confusion and seeming irrationality of the Supplementary Benefits scheme. Although not large in relation to the whole social security budget – accounting for only 18% of its expenditure – Supplementary Benefit was a system of fundamental importance, responsible for maintaining the income of some eight million people at the poverty line through a maze of investigation, rules and regulations that required the employment of nearly a half of the staff of the DHSS to operate. The stigma of Supplementary Benefit and the complexity of its procedures meant, moreover, that an estimated one-quarter of those without employment living below the poverty line failed to claim the benefit for which they were eligible.

The response of the government was to propose what it argued would be a simpler and clearer system, but it was to be one in which significant groups of claimants would lose considerably. On the basis of an argument that the complexity of the previous system resulted from an attempt to tailor benefits to the needs of individual claimants – a practice that was suitable to an era of residual poverty, but unworkable in the new era of large-scale poverty – payments under the Income Support scheme would in future be made not on the basis of individual need but on the basis of broad claimant groups.

The first distinction to be made was one of age, with single, childless claimants only eligible for the standard rate of Income Support once they reached the age of 25. Until then they receive only the rate normally paid to non-householder dependants. For those who qualify for the full rate, the previous payment of a higher long-term rate of benefit to pensioners, the sick or single parents and the weekly discretionary additions to benefit for particular claimants were both abolished, and replaced by a weekly premium paid on top of the standard rate of Income Support to those with families, the elderly, single parents and the chronic sick and disabled. The unemployed, previously debarred from receiving the higher rate of long-term benefit, were similarly to be denied a premium in their own right, no matter how long they remained on benefit, or how great their need.

The ending of the discretionary power to vary a claimant's benefit in accordance with need led to a serious loss of income, especially for those claimants such as the severely disabled whose needs were greater than other claimants. It also placed a lid on an area in which claimants had at least the possibility of influencing the payment they received. 'The aim', argued the report, 'will be to give claimants a reasonable level of help rather than to provide in detail for every variation in individual circumstances' (HMSO 1985:23). However, in a system where the level of support was to remain at subsistence level, the failure to take account of individual circumstances would for some mean an inadequate income and inevitable hardship.

For such claimants, the 1986 Social Security Act introduced the Social Fund. This fund, whose resources are set annually at a fixed level, provides loans for single items of expenditure at the discretion of special and separate Benefit Officers. There is, unlike the previous system of single payments which it replaced, no independent right of appeal against the refusal of such a loan, and any loan granted has to be repaid by the claimant through weekly deductions from benefit.

With the abolition of single payments the problem of

discretion had come full circle. Having encountered a system where the power to increase a claimant's benefit had provided claimants with a lever to extract higher levels of relief, the Conservative government in 1980 had sought to limit such pressure by the introduction of regulations specifying entitlement. The failure of this to have more than a short-term effect on the rising number of claims and payments led in 1986 to the abolition of such payments and their replacement by a fixed rate of benefit. The Social Fund, as the last resort of those for whom the fixed rate of benefit was insufficient, reintroduced discretion at its worst: as the arbitrary power of a separate and unaccountable group of officials to determine those who are deserving of help, and even then to provide them with a repayable loan that only leads them further into debt.

A continuing programme

In 1987, and in great part in face of an opposition that was in varying degrees discredited, demoralised, divided and in disarray, the Conservative government was returned for a third term of office, with expectations of continuing its radical programme of reforming British society. The vision of society embodied in such a programme, and the means of achieving it, fundamentally challenge many of the taken-for-granted assumptions of the post-war era. The costs and risks in doing so are immense.

At one level this agenda has had a clear material foundation. In the short term at least the economic crisis of capitalism has been met by attempts to reduce wage costs and the living standards of a large part of the population, and thus to restore the profitability of private capital. As a long-term strategy, however, it reveals a myopia that threatens a continuing decline of large areas of the British economy into a low-wage, low-technology assembly branch for international capital, and in which a large number of insecure and low-paid workers service the needs of an affluent minority.

Within such an agenda, the young – and working class and black youth in particular – are a singular target (see Davies 1986). Highly visible in their culture and life-styles, shunned by employers for their lack of discipline and commitment in favour of the employment of more constrained groups of workers such as married women, threatening inner-city riots, or simply standing around on the streets or in shopping centres, the assault on the expectations, the wages, and even the very visibility of young people has grown with increasing ferocity.

Since the beginning of the 1980s Conservative ministers and others have argued, in spite of the evidence, that young people had 'priced themselves out of work', that their unemployment was a result of their own making, and that the only solution was for them to reduce their expectations and take whatever work was available. The activities of the Manpower Services Commission, with its series of work experience programmes and temporary job creation schemes was to be an important part of this pressure, exposing a whole generation to an initial experience of work and training that was non-unionised, unprotected by health and safety or anti-discriminatory legislation, low-paid, and increasingly determined by the needs and wishes of employers (see Benn and Fairley 1986). To this was added the removal of young people from the minimum wage protection of the Wages Councils, subsidies to employers who took on young people at particularly low rates of pay, cuts in benefit available to unemployed youth, and in the 1986 Social Security Act the raising of the age for adult benefit to 25 (see Allbeson 1985).

Other aspects of youth policy were even more draconian. In 1985, for example, the government introduced new regulations limiting the length of time for which single homeless unemployed people under the age of 26 could claim benefit for board and lodgings accommodation. A maximum period of entitlement was set, ranging between two and eight weeks in different parts of the country – 'a reasonable time', argued the Minister for Social Security, 'for the sort of job search which all of us are anxious to encourage' (*Hansard* 21st March 1985). Introduced on the spurious justification that unemployed youngsters and adults were abusing the system by living in seaside resorts at the taxpayers' expense, the regulations went on to limit payments in all areas of the country, including a claimant's home town, thus forcing the homeless young unemployed back into their parents' home where this was possible, and where not either to sleep rough or to move every few weeks from one part of the country to another in order to claim.

In 1984 there had been 37,000 people under the age of 26 living in bed and breakfast or hostel accommodation – an increase from 23,000 only two years earlier, and a reflection of the growing extent of homelessness. In relation to the total number of young people the numbers thus affected are only a small minority (although they are no less severely affected for that). Yet the message to working class youth in general is clear: to expect no mercy and consideration from the hands of the state. Furthermore, as *The Times* pointed out, such moves were 'more important for the long run, to establish the violability of basic social benefits and do it for a group over which the political screams will not be too loud' (cited Allbeson 1985:86).

In point of fact, the screams were loud, and the government was involved in considerable embarrassment and delay in pushing the legislation through. The removal of benefit entitlement, however, not only from the homeless but from young people in general remains a persistent part of the Tory agenda. As Margaret Thatcher has argued:

> Unemployment should not be an option ... It's too easy for some of them, straight out of school, to go straight onto social security at the age of 16. They like it, they have a lot of money, and some of them learn a way of life they should never have a chance to learn.

> (Cited Allbeson 1985:90)

With cuts in educational provision adding to Britain's place at the bottom of the ladder in terms of the proportion of young people in advanced industrialised societies staying on in education beyond the age of 16, the alternatives for young people are few. Either they must depend upon their families, or else seek work in the low-paid service sector of the economy which right-wing economists and politicians have argued will materialise once wage levels have been reduced. It is 'from the McDonalds and Wimpys' argues Margaret Thatcher, 'from the kind of Disneyland they are starting at Corby' that the new jobs are to come (cited *Sunday Times* 15/4/84).

Like the young, the long-term unemployed have similarly become a target for government attention. Indeed, given the collapse in job opportunities for young people, the young also count for a significant proportion of those unemployed for a year or more, and in a static labour market their prospects of returning to employment diminish the longer they remain unemployed. Long-term unemployment remains as a major factor in the incidence of poverty, yet the solutions offered by the Conservative government have been again to seek to limit benefit payments and exert financial and other pressures on the unemployed in the belief that work will be available once expectations have been sufficiently reduced. The introduction of subsidies to low-wage employment, such as the Jobstart allowance has been one aspect of this strategy. So too has been increased testing of the unemployed's availability for work, with women particularly subject to attempts to discourage them from active participation in the labour market. Additionally, under such initiatives as the Restart programme, as well as the continuing work of unemployment review officers, all of the long-term unemployed are put under scrutiny and increasing pressure in their attempts to find work. But in the absence of employment opportunities, especially of a sort that would provide an adequate standard of living, pressure on the unemployed to leave the benefit register only further increases the depth and extent of poverty.

That much of the cost of this is borne by families places an increasing burden in particular on women, who, whether as unemployed, as the majority of workers in low-paid jobs, as carers for dependants or as old age pensioners carry the brunt of the burden of poverty. This feminisation of poverty – according to the 1985 Family Expenditure Survey, for example, single women account for 63% of the very poor – is not solely a product of Thatcherism, but also reflects longer-term economic and demographic trends. Yet far even from recognising it as a problem, government policies have served to confirm and exacerbate it.

In other aspects of policy, attention has been directed not so much at people's expectations of work and wages, but at their expectations of the state. As Chris Jones (1983b) has argued, the attempt to reduce people's expectations of and demands on the state, to de-politicise social and economic life, goes a long way to explain the right's stress on the privatisation of public industries and services and its desire to reduce if not abolish the welfare functions of the state.

This much was evident in the Conservative government's ill-fated proposal of 1985 to abolish SERPS, the State Earnings Related Pension Scheme. Introduced originally by a Labour government in 1978 in an attempt to gain a consensus between the political parties and between trade unions and employers over the future of pensions provision, SERPS was an attempt to do something about poverty in old age that ended up highly compromised. Nevertheless, although it allowed workers and their employers to 'contract out' of the state scheme by making their own private pension provision, for that half of the population not covered by private pension schemes, SERPS was to provide an important earnings-related supplement to the basic state pension. Based as it was on the best twenty years rather than on lifetime earnings, it was of particular benefit to manual workers (whose earnings tend to decline as they get older) and to women and others with more intermittent employment.

The abolition of SERPS had formed the centrepiece of the government's proposals for the 1986 Social Security Act. Arguing that it constituted a commitment which, with the growing proportion of elderly people in the population, future generations would be both unable and unwilling to support, the Fowler review proposed its replacement by a compulsion on all workers to take out a private pension scheme which would provide a pension based on the amount of money paid in. Apart from the even greater inequalities that this would produce in old age, the shift from state to private provision of pensions, even accepting the government's predictions and description of the elderly as a growing 'burden', would not solve the problem. As the *Financial Times* pointed out, 'this burden will be a problem for the future economy however pensions are financed'. Indeed, the cost of privatising pensions would be greater, since under the state scheme the cost of administering SERPS amounted to less than 1 per cent of benefits; within the private sector the cost of administration, profit and dividends average a significant 20 per cent.

The clearly ideological attempt of the government to abolish SERPS, carried on against the advice of its own appointed experts, and thus to remove the state from a responsibility to ensure against poverty in old age, was finally to be defeated by the weight of opposition not only from the pensioners' movement and other allied supporters, but even from the employers' CBI and the private pensions industry. In its final form, the 1986 Social Security Act introduced a series of modifications, cutting the pension paid from 25% to 20% of earnings and replacing the 20-year calculation with one based on lifetime earnings. It remains for future pensioners a significant blow, but for the government it represented a major defeat.

The two-thirds society

The change in the structure of employment and in the operation of the labour market that is taking place in the last quarter of the twentieth century – the growth of casual labour of various sorts, accompanied by large-scale and chronic unemployment – is not the temporary effect of a capitalist economy in recession. It is a process that has accelerated and been brought to a new height by economic slump and by a political intervention that have combined to weaken workers' ability to resist. But it is a trend which, in seeking to break the economic and political strength of labour, has been in development since the height of the post-war boom.

Nor is it a trend that is likely to disappear with economic recovery and growth. On the contrary, economic growth is likely to confirm and exacerbate such changes rather than confront them. Thus the growth of the British economy during the mid-1980s at an annual rate of 2–3% failed to have any appreciable effect on levels of unemployment, while at the same time it saw more permanent jobs replaced by casual labour. Internationally, the increased mobility of capital makes it less reliant on any one national economy or labour force, and able to replicate and demand similar conditions elsewhere. The post-war era of 'full' employment in the advanced capitalist economies is ended, at least for the foreseeable future.

One effect of these changes has been to create a sharp increase in poverty. This has been true not only for those rejected from the labour market, but also for a rising number of those employed within it. This trend towards growing and large-scale poverty is similarly unlikely to be reversed.

Another effect has been to draw out and exacerbate lines of cleavage within the working class. Economic polarisation has been accompanied by growing geographical, social and political division. These lines of division are not of course new. Even during the era of supposed 'full' employment, not everyone who wanted one could find a job. Still less did full employment mean that those who did find work – particularly black workers who were encouraged to migrate to Britain or the increasing number of women employed – could also find adequate wages and security. Nor did full employment eradicate the poverty facing many pensioners, single parents or others outside of the labour market. As the 'rediscovery' of poverty in the midst of the so-called affluent society of the 1950s and 1960s showed, poverty is an enduring feature of capitalism, both in and out of work, through boom and slump alike.

Yet the increase in poverty that has come with the end of the post-war boom has been accompanied by a growing polarisation. Rather than closing, as they did, although only slightly, in the post-war decades up until the 1970s, these lines of cleavage are being widened. The divisions, not only between rich and poor, but within the working class itself – in terms of age, race, gender, skill or geography – are being drawn much more sharply.

The new right has built upon these divisions. Its appeal has been to the more affluent and protected: not just to employers and the wealthy, but also to white collar workers and the skilled working class. It has sought to extend the private provision of welfare as a fringe benefit to certain workers, while it has denigrated state provision as unproductive and as a burden on those in work, although it has been careful not to attack too directly those state welfare services on which the more powerful most depend. It has offered tax-cuts to those with above-average incomes, whilst reducing the social wage of the poorest. The pursuit of individual gain and self-interest has been promoted above the values, however imperfectly they were realised in the post-war welfare state, of creating a more equal, inclusive and compassionate society.

In an increasingly divided society, the new right has sought to create the conditions where it can gain sufficient electoral support from amongst the more prosperous and powerful two-thirds of society: a population that is mostly in employment, relatively secure and largely white. There is of course little that is new in this. Yet one of the most distinctive features of Thatcherism has been its willingness to abandon any pretence of concern or responsibility for the remainder. It has purposefully rejected the pursuit of greater equality and actively encouraged the growth of social division.

Meanwhile the remaining third – and in particular working class youth, many black people, the unemployed and other groups amongst the poor – are subjected to increased policing and surveillance, not least by a welfare system that increasingly gives up its pretensions towards achieving greater equality and fairness in favour of a role emphasising discipline and constraint. An acceptance of the growth and permanence of poverty has necessitated a response which seeks to suppress and contain its more threatening social and political consequences.

The system of social security has been used to play a major part in this creation of a more coercive social policy and a more authoritarian state. In its dealings with an underclass of black claimants, the long-term unemployed, working class youth and those who compete in the growing casual labour market, without the protection of trades unions or the support of mainstream political organisations, it has adopted a more rigid and punitive stance. In its assault on the notion of a right to benefits, its increasing pressure on the unemployed, its resistance to the expectations and demands of the young or of women, and in its stigmatisation of the poor it has, along with other government measures, sought to assist in the creation of a less secure and more vulnerable workforce that the changing demands of capital in the last quarter of the twentieth century require.

In doing this the social security system does no more than it has always done. Throughout its history its primary role has been to uphold the operation of a capitalist labour market, with its social and sexual divisions of labour, and to control and contain the inequalities and poverty that result. In the course of its history the state has at times had to respond flexibly to the political challenge created by poverty. But the social security system has never been intended to abolish poverty, nor has it been capable of doing so. The centrality of poverty to capitalism, and the importance of social security as a means of maintaining poverty and of 'moralising' and regulating the poor, has and will always set the limits of its operation.

BIBLIOGRAPHY

Place of publication is London, unless otherwise given.

Anon. Socialism and self-help. (1889). *London Quarterly Review* 72.

Abrams, P. (1968). *The Origins of British Sociology*. University of Chicago Press.

Adams, W.S. (1953). 'Lloyd George and the labour movement'. *Past and Present* 3.

Alden, P. (1905). *The Unemployed: A National Question*. P.S. King.

Alden, P. (1908). *The Unemployable and the Unemployed*. Headley Bros.

Allbeson, J. (1985). 'Seen but not heard: young people'. In S. Ward (ed) 'DHSS in crisis'. CPAG *Poverty Pamphlet* 66.

Anderson, P. (1966). 'Origins of the present crisis'. In Anderson, P. and Blackburn, R. *Towards Socialism*. Collins.

Arnold, A. (1888). 'Socialism and the unemployed.' *Contemporary Review* 53.

Arnold, M. (1880). 'The Future of Liberalism'. *Nineteenth Century* VIII.

Atherley-Jones, L.A. (1893). 'Liberalism and social reform: a warning'. *The New Review* 9.

Bailward, W. (1907). 'The Charity Organisation Society'. *Quarterly Review* 206.

Ball, S. (1906). 'The moral aspects of socialism'. *Fabian Tract* 72.

Benn, C. and Fairley, J. (1986). *Challenging the MSC*. Pluto Press.

Beveridge, W.H. (1904a). 'The vagrant and the unemployable'. *Toynbee Record*. April.

Beveridge, W.H. (1904b). 'The making of paupers'. *Toynbee Record* Nov.

Beveridge, W.H. (1904c). 'Unemployment in London: the preservation of efficiency'. *Toynbee Record*, December.

Beveridge, W.H. (1905). 'The question of disenfranchisement'. *Toynbee Record* March.

Beveridge, W.H. (1906). 'The problem of the unemployed'. *Sociological Papers* III.

Beveridge, W.H. (1907). 'Labour exchanges and the unemployed'. *Economic Journal* 17, 65.

Beveridge, W.H. (1908). 'Unemployment and its cure: the first step'. *The Contemporary Review* 93.

Beveridge, W.H. (1909 and 1930). *Unemployment: A Problem of Industry.* Longmans Green & Co.

Beveridge, W.H. (1944). *Full Employment in a Free Society.* George Allen & Unwin.

Bonner, A. (1961). *British Co-operation: The History, Principles and Organisation of the British Co-operative Movement.* Co-operative Union, Manchester.

Booth, C. (1904). *Life and Labour of the People in London.* Vol 1. Macmillan.

Bosanquet, H. (*née* Dendy) (1893). 'The industrial residuum'. *Economic Journal* III.

Bosanquet, H. (1896). *The Rich and the Poor.* Macmillan.

Bowley, M. (1949). *Nassau Senior and Classical Economics.* Augustus Kelly. New York.

Braithwaite, W. (1957). *Lloyd George's Ambulance Wagon.* Cedric Chivers, Bath.

Briggs E. and Deacon A. (1973). 'The creation of the Unemployment Assistance Board'. *Policy and Politics.* 2.

Brown, J. (1964). *Ideas Concerning Social Policy and their Influence on Legislation in Britain 1902-1911.* Unpublished PhD Thesis. University of London.

Brown, J. (1968). 'Charles Booth and the labour colonies 1889-1905'. *Economic History Review* XII. 2.

Brown, K. (1971). *Labour and Unemployment.* Rowman & Littlefield.

Burleigh, B. (1887). 'The unemployed'. *Contemporary Review* LII.

Burns, J. (1906). 'The unemployed'. *Fabian Tract* 47.

Calder, A. (1971). *The People's War.* Panther.

Caldwell, J. (1959). 'The genesis of the Ministry of Labour'. *Public Administration* 37.

Castles, S. (1984). *Here For Good: Western Europe's New Ethnic Minorities.* Pluto Press.

Chamberlain, J. (1892). 'Old age pensions and friendly societies'. *The National Review* 24.

Charity Organisation Society (1908). *Report of the Special Committee on Unskilled Labour.* C.O.S.

Churchill, W.S. (1909). *Liberalism and the Social Problem.* Hodder &

Stoughton.

Churchill, R.S. (1967). *Winston S. Churchill* (Vol II – Young Statesman 1901–14). Heinemann.

Churchill, R.S. (1969). *Winston S. Churchill* (Vol II Companion Pt 2. 1907–11). Heinemann.

Cooper, S. (1985). 'Observations in Supplementary Benefit Offices'. *The Reform of Supplementary Benefit*. Working Paper C. Policy Studies Institute.

Corrigan, P. (1977). *State Formation and Moral Regulation in Nineteenth Century Britain*. Unpublished PhD Thesis. University of Durham.

Cromwell, V. (1966). 'Interpretations of nineteenth century administration'. *Victorian Studies* 9.

Davidson, R. (1971). *Sir Hubert Llewellyn Smith and Labour Policy 1886–1916*. Unpublished PhD Thesis. University of Cambridge.

Davies, B. (1986). *Threatening Youth*. Open University Press. Milton Keynes.

Davin, A. (1978). 'Imperialism and Motherhood'. *History Workshop* 5.

Dawson, W.H. (1891). *Bismarck and State Socialism*. Swan Sonnenschein.

Deacon, A. (1976). *In Search of the Scrounger*. Social Administration Research Trust.

Digby, A. (1975). 'The labour market and the continuity of social policy after 1834'. *Economic History Review*. XXVIII. 1.

Eden, Sir F.M. (1796). *The State of the Poor: Or, an History of the Labouring Classes in England*. (Rep. Cass 1966).

Extracts From the Information Received by His Majesty's Commission. 1837.

Fabian Society (1886). *The Government Organisation of Unemployed Labour*. Standring.

Feinstein, C.H. (1968). 'Changes in the distribution of the national income in the United Kingdom since 1860'. In Marchal, J. and Ducros, B. *The Distribution of the National Income*. Macmillan.

Finer, S.E. (1952). *The Life and Times of Sir Edwin Chadwick*. Methuen.

Fraser, D. (1973). *The Evolution of the British Welfare State*. Macmillan.

Freedan, M. (1972). *English Liberal Thought: Problems of Social Reform 1886–1914*. Unpublished PhD Thesis. University of Oxford.

Fryer, P. (1984). *Staying Power: the History of Black People in Britain*. Pluto Press.

Furniss, E.S. (1965). *The Position of the Labourer in a System of Nationalism, (1918)*. Augustus M. Kelley. New York.

Gallacher, W. (1951). *Rise Like Lions*. Lawrence & Wishart.

Gates, P. (1910). 'Unemployment': Paper read to the Conference of the Charity Organisation Society.

Gennard, J. and Lasko, R. (1974). 'Supplementary Benefits and strikers'. *British Journal of Industrial Relations* 12.

Gilbert, B. (1964). 'The decay of nineteenth century provident institutions and the coming of old age pensions'. *Economic History Review* XVII. 3.

Gilbert, B. (1966a). 'Winston Churchill versus the Webbs: the origins of British unemployment insurance'. *American Historical Review* 71, 3.

Gilbert, B. (1966b). *The Evolution of National Insurance in Great Britain.* Michael Joseph.

Gilroy, P. (1987). *There Ain't No Black in the Union Jack: The Cultural Politics of Race and Nation.* Hutchinson.

Gosden, P.H. (1973). *Self Help: Voluntary Associations in the Nineteenth Century.* Batsford.

Halevy, E. (1951). *The Growth of Philosophic Radicalism.* Faber.

Hammond, J.L. and B. (1913). *The Village Labourer 1760–1832.* Longmans, Green & Co.

Hannington, W. (1936). *Unemployed Struggles.* Lawrence & Wishart.

Hannington, W. (1978). *Ten Lean Years* (1940). EP Publishing. Wakefield.

Hardwick, C. (1869). *The History, Present Position and Social Importance of Friendly Societies.* Heywood. Manchester.

Harris, J. (1972). *Unemployment and Politics: A Study in English Social Policy 1886–1914.* Oxford University Press.

Hasbach W. (1908). *A History of the English Agricultural Labourer.* P.S. King.

Hill, C. (1952). 'Puritans and the poor'. *Past and Present* 2.

H.M.S.O. (1942). *Social Insurance and Allied Services* (The Beveridge Report). Cmd 6404.

H.M.S.O. (1985). *The Reform of Social Security* Vols I and II. Cmnd 9517/8.

Hobsbawm, E. (1967). 'Custom, wages and work-load in nineteenth century industry'. In Briggs, A. and Saville, J. *Essays in Labour History.* Macmillan.

Hobsbawm, E. (1974). *Industry and Empire.* Pelican.

Hobson, J.A. (1895). 'The meaning and measure of "unemployment"'. *Contemporary Review* 67.

Hobson, J.A. (1896). 'Is poverty diminishing?' *Contemporary Review* April.

Hollis, P. (1970). *The Pauper Press: A Study in Working Class Radicalism of the 1830s.* Oxford University Press.

Hollis, P. (1973). *Class and Conflict in Nineteenth Century England 1815–1850.* Routledge & Kegan Paul.

Holyoake, J.G. (1878). 'The new principle of industry'. *Nineteenth Century* 4.

Hutchinson, J. (1908). 'A workman's view of the remedy for unemployment'. *Nineteenth Century* 64.

Hutson, T. (1943). 'Social security and assistance'. Public Records Office file PIN 8/12.

Jackson, C. (1910). *Unemployment and Trade Unions.* Longmans Green & Co.

Jackson, C. and Pringle, J. (1909). 'The effects of employment or assistance given to the unemployed since 1886'. In *Report . . .* (1909) Appendix Vol XII.

Jones, C. (1975). *'The reserve army of labour: a search for solutions'.* Paper presented to the University of Durham Political Economy Group.

Jones, C. (1976). 'The foundations of social work education'. *Working Papers in Sociology* 11. University of Durham.

Jones, C. (1978). *An Analysis of the Development of Social Work and Social Work Education 1869–1977.* Unpublished PhD Thesis. University of Durham.

Jones, C. (1983). *State Social Work and the Working Class.* Macmillan.

Jones, C. (1983b). 'Thatcherism and the attack on expectations'. *Bulletin on Social Policy* 14. Rochdale.

Jones, C. and Novak, T. (1985). 'Welfare against the workers: benefits as a political weapon'. In H. Beynon (ed) *Digging Deeper: Issues in the Miners' Strike.* Verso.

Kay-Shuttleworth, Sir J.P.B. (1832). *The Moral and Physical Condition of the Working Classes Employed in the Cotton Manufacture in Manchester.* Frank Cass. 1970.

Kincaid, J. (1973). *Poverty and Equality in Britain.* Penguin.

Kirkman-Gray, B. (1908). *Philanthropy and the State.* P.S. King.

Langan M. and Schwarz B. (1985). *Crises in the British State.* Hutchinson/CCCS.

Lansbury, G. (1903). *The Principles of the English Poor Law.* T.U.C.

Lenin, V.I. (1965). *Imperialism: The Highest Stage of Capitalism.* Foreign Languages Press. Peking.

Levy, S.L. (1970). *Nassau W. Senior.* David & Charles. Newton Abbot.

Lewis, F.W. (1909). *State Insurance: A Social and Industrial Need.* Archibald Constable.

Llewellyn Smith, Sir H. (1910). 'Economic security and unemployment insurance'. *Economic Journal* XX.

Lloyd George, D. (1910). *The Problem of Unemployment.* Liberal Publications Department.

Lloyd George, D. (1911). *The People's Insurance.* Hodder & Stoughton.

Lynd, H.M. (1943). *England in the Eighteen-Eighties.* Oxford University Press.

McGregor, O.R. (1957). 'Social research and social policy in the nineteenth century'. *British Journal of Sociology* 8.

MacKay, T. (1902). 'The poor law and the economic order'. *Economic Review* 12.

Mandel, E. (1968). *Marxist Economic Theory.* Merlin.

Marshall, D. (1926). *The English Poor in the Eighteenth Century.* George Rutledge.

Marx, K. (1973). *Grundrisse.* Pelican.

Marx, K. (1974). *Capital* Vol I. Lawrence & Wishart.

Marx, K. and Engels, F. (1968). *Selected Works.* Lawrence & Wishart.

Marx, K. and Engels, F. (1975). *Articles on Britain.* Progress Publishers. Moscow.

Mencher, S. (1961). 'The changing basis of status and contract in assistance policy'. *Social Service Review* March.

Miliband, R. and Liebman, M. (1985/6). 'Beyond social democracy'. *Socialist Register.*

Millett, J.D. (1940). *The Unemployment Assistance Board.* George Allen & Unwin.

Moore, B. (1969). *Social Origins of Dictatorship and Democracy.* Peregrine.

Morton, A.L. and Tate, G. (1956). *The British Labour Movement.* Lawrence & Wishart.

Nairn, T. (1972). 'The English working class'. In R. Blackburn (ed) *Ideology and Social Science.* Fontana.

Navarro, V. (1982). 'The crisis of the international capitalist order.' *Critical Social Policy* 2, 1.

Nicolaus, M. (1967). 'Proletariat and middle class in Marx'. *Studies on the Left* 7.

Novak, T. (1984). *Poverty and Social Security.* Pluto Press.

Pelling, H. (1968). *Popular Politics and Society in Late Victorian Britain.* Macmillan.

Phillipson, C. (1982). *Capitalism and the Construction of Old Age.* Macmillan.

Pinker, R. (1973). *Social Theory and Social Policy.* Heinemann.

Pollard, S. (1963). 'Factory discipline in the industrial revolution'. *Economic History Review* 16.

Pound, J. (1973). *Poverty and Vagrancy in Tudor England.* Longman.

Powell, E. (1972). *Still To Decide.* Batsford.

Poynter, J.R. (1969). *Society and Pauperism: English Ideas on Poor Relief 1795–1834.* Routledge & Kegan Paul.

Rae, J. (1890). 'State socialism and social reform'. *Contemporary Review* 58.

Rea, R. (1912). *Social Reform Versus Socialism.* Liberal Publications Department.

Reid, G. (1948). The Assistance Board. Public Records Office File PIN 8/12.

Redford, A. (1964). *Labour Migration in England 1800–50* (1926). Manchester University Press.

Report of His Majesty's Commission for Inquiring Into the Administration and Practical Operation of the Poor Laws 1834 (Reprinted with an introduction by S. and E. Checkland. Penguin, 1975).

Report of the Royal Commission on the Poor Laws and the Relief of Distress (1909). (3 vols). Cd 4499.

Report of the Committee on Abuse of Social Security Benefits (1973). Cmnd 6615.

Richards, P. (1975). *The State and the Working Class: Private MPs and Social Policy in the 1830s*. Unpublished PhD Thesis. University of Birmingham.

Rodgers, B. (1969). *The Battle Against Poverty* (2 vols). Routledge & Kegan Paul.

Rose, M.E. (1966). 'The anti-Poor Law movement in the North of England'. *Northern History* 1.

Rose, M.E. (1971). *The English Poor Law 1780-1930*. David & Charles.

Rothstein, T. (1929). *From Chartism to Labourism*. Martin Lawrence.

Saville, J. (1957). 'The welfare state: an historical approach'. *The New Reasoner*.

Saville, J. (1969). 'Primitive accumulation and early industrialisation in Britain'. *Socialist Register*.

de Schweinitz, K. (1947). *England's Road to Social Security 1349-1947*. University of Pennsylvania.

Searle, G. (1971). *The Quest for National Efficiency*. Blackwell. Oxford.

Semmel, B. (1960). *Imperialism and Social Reform: 1895-1914*. George Allen & Unwin.

Senior, N.W. (1865). *Historical and Philosophical Essays*. Longmans Green & Co.

Sires, R. (1955). 'Labour unrest in England'. *Journal of Economic History* XV, 3.

Sklar, H. (1980). *Trilateralism*. South End Press, Boston.

Smart, W. (1909). 'The first six years of the Local Government Board: the crusade against outdoor relief'. In *Report ... 1909* Appendix Vol XII.

Social Assistance: A Review of the Supplementary Benefits Scheme in Great Britain 1978, D.H.S.S.

Stedman Jones, G. (1971). *Outcast London: A Study in the Relationship Between Classes in Victorian Society*. Oxford University Press.

Supple, B. (1974). 'Legislation and virtue: an essay on working class self-help and the state in the early nineteenth century'. In McKendrick, N. (ed) *Historical Perspectives*. Europa.

Sweezy, P. (1946). *The Theory of Capitalist Development*. Dennis Dobson.

Thane, P. (n.d.). 'The working class and the origins of the welfare state'. Unpublished paper.

Thompson, D. (1957). 'The welfare state'. *The New Reasoner*.

Thompson, E.P. (1965). 'The peculiarities of the English'. *Socialist Register*.

Thompson, E.P. (1967). 'Time, work discipline and industrial capitalism'. *Past and Present* 38.

Thompson, E.P. (1971). 'The moral economy of the English crowd in the eighteenth century'. *Past and Present* 50.

Thompson, E.P. (1974). *The Making of the English Working Class*. Penguin.

Townsend, P. and Davidson, N. (1982). *Inequalities In Health: The Black Report*. Penguin.

Treble, J. (1970). 'The attitudes of the friendly societies towards the movement in Great Britain for state pensions 1878–1908'. *International Review of Social History* 15.

Walley, Sir J. (1972). *Social Security: Another British Failure?* C. Knight.

Webb, S. (1890). 'The reform of the Poor Law'. *Contemporary Review* 58.

Webb, S. (1906). 'Twentieth century politics: a policy of national efficiency'. *Fabian Tract* 108.

Webb, S. (1910/11). 'Eugenics and the Poor Law: the Minority Report'. *Eugenic Review* 2, 3.

Webb, S. and B. (1929). *English Local Government: Part II* (2 vols). Longmans Green & Co.

Wilson, E. (1977). *Women and the Welfare State*. Tavistock.

Wilson, E. (1980). *Only Halfway to Paradise: Women in Postwar Britain 1945–1968*. Tavistock.

Winter, J.M. (1974). *Socialism and the Challenge of War*. Routledge & Kegan Paul.

Wohl, A.S. (1968). 'The bitter cry of outcast London'. *International Review* XII.

Wootton, B. (1944). *Social Security and the Beveridge Plan*. Common Wealth.

Young, N. (1967). 'Prometheans or troglodytes: the English working class and the dialectics of incorporation'. *Berkeley Journal of Sociology* 12.

Youngjohns, B. (1954). 'Co-operation and the state 1814–1914'. *Co-operative College Papers* March.

Index